© Copyright: A Guide To Information and Resources
3rd Edition

© Copyright: A Guide To Information and Resources, 3rd Edition

Gary H. Becker, Consultant

P.O. Box 951870

Lake Mary, FL 32795-1870

888-333-2037

gbecker@earthlink.net

INTRODUCTION

The purpose of this guide is to provide a day-to-day copyright reference for educators, trainers, librarians, media staffs and technology support personnel.

This guide is a product of extensive research into the law, court cases and respected legal opinions. However, it does not constitute legal advice.

It is important to note that as with many laws, the writers are the best source of the intent of the legislation. Much of the interpretation of the law is based upon the House and Senate versions of the Copyright Act prior to its formal adoption as well as the Congressional discussions that have led to amendments/modifications since that time. The courts, in making their decisions as to possible copyright infringement, refer to the Congressional Reports for clarification of legislative intent. For those individuals desiring a more in-depth knowledge of Copyright Law, or the basis for some of the guidelines included in this manual, reference citations are provided.

However, all is not absolute. The Copyright Law weighs, in balance, the rights of the author and the needs of society. The law grants the author certain exclusive rights and protections, for a limited period of time, while recognizing the need for society to have access to these materials. This has led to formalizing, in the law, the concept of Fair Use, which places some limitations on the exclusive rights of authors.

Gary H. Becker
Consultant

2003

©Microsoft Clip Art

Table of Contents

Quick Reference 1

Chapter 1 - Items Protected/Not Protected 8
What is Copyright? 8
What Is Protected Under Copyright? 8
What Is Not Protected Under Copyright? 9

Chapter 2 - Fair Use 10
Criteria & Guidelines 10
   The Functional Test 11
   Satire, Burlesque and Parody 11
   Incidental Reproduction 11
   Other Fair Use Applications 11

Chapter 3 - Photocopying 13
Teacher/Classroom Photocopying 13
Library Photocopying 14
   Systematic Reproduction 15
   Rights Of Reproduction Do Not Apply To: 16
Library Photocopying for Reserve Use 16
Library Photocopying for Interlibrary Loan 17
Photocopying of Out-of-Print Materials 18
Facsimile Reproduction (Fax Copying) 18
Fair Use Questions/Situations 19
   Making "Big Books" 19
   Sharing Resources Via Fax 19
   Presenters Copying and Distributing Articles 19
   Black-line Master Books 20
   Reproducing Out-of-Print Materials 20
   Reprinting Current News Articles for Classroom Use 20

Chapter 4 - Public Performance 21
Public Performance In A Classroom 21
Public Performance In A Library 22

Public Performance At School Assemblies 23
Performance By Non-profit Veterans or Fraternal Organizations 23

Chapter 5 - Music 24
Permissible Uses 24
Prohibitions 25
Other Considerations.. 25
Fair Use Questions/Situations 26
   Reproducing Sheet Music for Extra Sections 26
   Reproducing Sheet Music for a Performance 26

Chapter 6 - Audiovisual Works 27
Permissible Uses 27
Prohibitions 27
Fair Use Questions/Situations 28
   Reading Stories Onto Tape/CD 28
   Copying/Reproducing Photographs 28
   Tracing Cartoon Characters 29
   Converting Records to Tape or CD's 29

Chapter 7 - Video 30
Off-air Videotaping 30
   Institutional Taping 30
   At Home for Institutional Use 32
   Taping From Cable and Satellite 32
Closed Circuit Television Transmissions 33
Using Copyrighted Videocassettes/DVD's With The "Home Use Only"
Warning Label (Schools & Libraries) 34
   Licensing Sources for Public Performance in Schools/Public Libraries....... 35
Instructional Broadcasting 35
   Transmission/Performance 36
   Transmission/Performance to Handicapped 37
   Recordings Made of Instructional Transmissions 37
   Recordings Made of Transmissions to Handicapped Individuals 38
Fair Use Questions/Situations 38
   Use of Donated Video Programs 38
   Conversion of Video Formats 38
   Use of Free Loan Video Rental Programs 39
   Use of Rental Video Programs in the Classroom 39
   Teacher Rental and Use of Video Program in Classroom 39

Videotaping Students Performing Copyrighted Works 40
Production and Sale of Original Drama Production 40
How to Use A Video Program for Entertainment, Reward, Motivation 41
Guest Presenters and Video Use Rights In The Classroom 41
Loan of Video Programs Between Schools 42
Use of Video Programs on Closed Circuit Systems 42
Taping and Redistribution of Satellite Programs 42
Demonstration of Digital Special Effects 42
Modifying a Sound Track to Accompany a Play 43
Use of Foreign, Copyrighted Video Programs 43
Students Taping From Cable For Use In Classroom 43
Use of PTA Purchased Videos For Reward/Instruction 43
Student Absence During 10 Day Use Period of Off-Air Programs 44
Digitizing Video Sources and Placing on a Digital, Video Server 44
Home Use vs. School Version Video Programs for Instructional Use 44
Creating a Satire of a Television Show or Commercial 45
Using Copyrighted Music on a Cable Access Channel 45
Using School Owned Videos in After School Programs 45

Chapter 8 - Computer Software and Applications 47

Duplication 47
   Converting Disk Programs To CD Format 48
   Transferring Programs To Hard Disk 48
Networking and Multiple Machine Loading 49
Use of Databases 49
   Downloading From Remote Databases 49
   Libraries - Creation and Distribution Of Digital Databases 50
   Libraries and Digital Reserves 51
Fair Use Questions/Situations 51
   Copying Programs for Home Use 51
   Making Copies By Backing Up Hard Drives 51
   Using Clip Art In A Student Newspaper That is Sold 52
   Placing Already Owned Programs On A Network 52
   Placing Programs On More Than One File Server 53
   Upgrading Software and Retaining Archival Copies 53
   Backup Of Lab Pack Software & Reproduction of Documentation 53
   Screen Capture From An On-Line Database Service 54
   Capturing Screen Images (Screen Dump) 54
   Reproducing Charts/Diagrams From A Computer Program 54
   Loading Personally Owned Software On School Computers 55
   Creating And Accessing A Library Database Program 55
   Developing Simulations/Tests Based Upon Copyrighted Content 55
   Installation of Donated Software on School Computers 55

Chapter 9 - Guidelines for Educational Multimedia 57

Guidelines As Different From Law 57
Preparation of Multimedia Projects Using Portions of Copyrighted Works.
.... 57
   By Students: 57
   By Educators: 57
Permitted Uses of Educational Multimedia Programs Created Under
These Guidelines 58
   Student Use: 58
   Educator Use for Curriculum-Based Instruction: 58
   Educator Use for Peer Conferences 58
   Educator Use for Professional Portfolio 59
Limitations - Time, Portion, Copying and Distribution 59
   Time Limitations 59
   Portion Limitations 59
   Motion Media 60
   Text Material 60
   Music, Lyrics and Music Video 60
   Illustrations and Photographs 60
   Numerical Data Sets 61
   Copying and Distribution Limitations 61
Examples of When Permission is Required 61
   Using Multimedia Projects for Non-Educational or Commercial Purposes .. 61
   Guidelines 61
   Distribution of Multimedia Projects Beyond Guidelines 61
Important Reminders 62
   Caution In Downloading Material From The Internet 62
   Attribution and Acknowledgment 62
   Notice of Use Restrictions 62
Future Uses Beyond Fair Use 63
   Duplication of Multimedia Projects Beyond Limitations Listed 63
   Integrity of Copyrighted Works: Alterations 63
   Reproduction or Decompilation of Copyrighted Computer Programs 63
   Licenses and Contracts 63
Fair Use Questions/Situations 63
   Modifying Scanned Or Digitized Images 63
   Use of Clip Art In Multimedia, Video and Computer Programs 64
   Importing Video Footage for a Quicktime Segment 64
   Using Text From Copyrighted Works 64
   Using Copyrighted Music In A Multimedia Production 64
   Using Photographs and Illustrations In A Powerpoint Presentation 65
   Using Information From Databases and Spreadsheets 65
   Permissible Copies of Finished, Multimedia Productions 65

Chapter 10 - DVD/CD-ROM & Laserdisc 66

CD-ROM Technology 66
DVD and Laserdisc Technology 67
Fair Use Questions/Situations 67
  Printing Articles From CD-ROM Encyclopedias & Periodicals 67
  Placing CD-ROM Resources On A Network 67

Chapter 11 - The Internet and Distance Learning 69

Guidelines for Use of the Internet 69
  Linking to Sites 69
  Website Creation and Ownership 70
Copyright and Distance Learning 70
  The TEACH Act 71
Fair Use Questions/Situations 72
  Reproducing A Newspaper Article Downloaded From A Web Site 72
  Forwarding Personal E-mail Messages 73
  Posting and E-Mailing Magazine Articles 73
  Use of Copyrighted Materials For Distance Learning 73
  Displaying Photographs, Charts, Tables 74
  Copying from the Internet to Make Class Copies 74
  Copying Graphics for Use on a Website 74

Chapter 12 - Obtaining Copyright Permission 75

Writing for Permission 75
  Copyright Searches 75
Licensing 76
Purchase Agreements 77

Chapter 13 - International Copyright 78

U.S. Joins Berne Union 78
Effect of U.S. Membership In The Berne Union 78
Subject Matter Protected By the Berne Convention 79
U.S. Law Amended 79
  Mandatory Notice of Copyright Is Abolished 79
  Mandatory Deposit 80
  Registration As A Prerequisite To A Law Suit* 80
General Agreement on Tariffs and Trade (GATT) 80
  Modification - Computer Software Rental Amendments Act28 80
  Protection for Live Performances 80
  Re-Establishes Protection for Foreign Works 81

Computer Programs and Compilations of Data 81
World Intellectual Property Treaty 81
Rights of Copyright Holders 81
Protection for Internet Service Providers/Carriers of Electronic Information
.... 81

Chapter 14 - Highlights of Law Changes and Court Decisions Affecting Education and Libraries 82

Encyclopedia Brittanica Educational Corp. vs. Crooks 1983 82
Brussels Satellite Convention - 1984 82
Berne Convention - 1989 82
Copyright Remedy Clarification Act - 1990 82
Computer Software Rental Amendments Act of 1990 83
Architectural Works Copyright Protection Act of 1990 83
Basic Books, Inc. vs. Kinko's Graphics Corp. - 1991 83
The Copyright Renewal Act of 1992 83
The Audio Home Recording Act of 1992 83
Fair Use - 1992 83
Copyright Reform Act of 1993 84
Satellite Home Viewer Act of 1994 84
Digital Performance Right In Sound Recordings Act 1995 84
American Geophysical Union vs. Texaco 84
Legislative Appropriations Act of 1997 84
World Intellectual Property Organization Treaty (WIPO) 85
Sonny Bono Copyright Term Extension Act 85
Digital Millennium Copyright Act 85
Digital Theft Deterrence and Copyright Damages Improvement Act of
1999 85
Work Made for Hire and Copyright Corrections Act of 2000 86
Technology, Education, and Copyright Harmonization Act of 2002
(TEACH Act) 86

Appendix A : Copyright Policies 87

Policy Development 87
Model Copyright Policy # 1 87
Model Copyright Policy # 2 88

Appendix B : Wording of Copyright Warning Notices 89

Warning In A Service Area 89
Warning In A Self-Service Area 89
General Warning 90

Appendix C : Sample Permissions Forms 91

Request for Off-Air Taping Within An Institution 91
Request To Duplicate Copyrighted Material 92
Request for Permission To Quote 93
Request to Use Rental Video In Classroom 94

Appendix D : Copyright Office Circulars & Factsheets .
.... 95

Internet and Fax on Demand 95

Glossary 97

Reference Citations 100

Bibliography 102

Books and Articles 102
Internet Resources 105
Associations Providing Copyright Information 107
United States Copyright Office 108
Copyright Cleared Production Music Libraries 110
Public Domain Music 111
Sources For Clip Art 112
Licensing/Performance Rights Agencies/Societies 113

Index 115

Quick Reference

This section should not be used as a substitute for the more complete information provided in this book, but rather as a refresher for day-to-day reference, once having become familiar with the contents of the following chapters.

Copyright Definition:	Copyright is a property right granted to authors, the purpose of which is to advance the public welfare by promoting artistic and scientific progress
Effective Date of the Law:	January 1, 1978
Length of Time Protected:	Works copyrighted prior to 1978: *28 years and renewal of 47 years*
	Works copyrighted in and after 1978: *Life of the author plus 70 years (If joint authors, life + 70 years of surviving author)*
Works Eligible for Protection:	Definition: Any tangible medium of expression, now known or later developed, which can be perceived, reproduced, or otherwise communicated, either with the aid of a machine or device....[1]
Author's Rights Protected:	Author has exclusive rights to do and authorize:[2] **(Also see definitions in Glossary)**

1. Reproduction of work
2. Prepare a derivative work based on copyrighted work
3. Distribution of the work by public sale, transfer of ownership or by rental lease or lending
4. Performance of the work publicly
5. Display of the work publicly

Liability:	$ 750.00 to $ 30,000 per infringement. If proven law broken by willful intent, statutory penalty may be raised to $ 150,000.

$ 500.00 to $ 250,000 per infringement and/or 1-5 years imprisonment if found guilty of willfully infringing the law for private or commercial gain.

Note: Court must waive statutory penalty of employee of a nonprofit educational institution or library where infringer can prove they believed they were operating under Fair Use interpretation. Does not eliminate possibility of a civil suit. [3]

Photocopying: (Single Copies) Teacher/Classroom Use
(See Chapter 3)

1. A chapter of a book
2. An article from a periodical or newspaper
3. A short story, short essay or short poem
4. A chart, diagram, cartoon or picture from a book, periodical or newspaper

Photocopying: (Multiple Copies) Teacher/Classroom Use
(See Chapter 3)

1. A complete poem if less than 250 words
2. An excerpt from a longer poem, not to exceed 250 words
3. A complete article, story or essay of less than 2500 words
4. Excerpt from a larger article, story or essay not to exceed 1,000 words or 10% of the whole, whichever is less
5. One chart, graph, diagram, carton or picture per book or periodical issue
6. Special works containing prose, poetry and illustrations, but limited to no more than 10% of the total

Limits to Preceding Photocopying:
(See Chapter 3)

1. Copying is made for one course only
2. One work from a single author
3. No more than 3 authors from a collective work
4. No more than 9 instances of multiple copying in one term
5. Copying does not replace or substitute for anthologies
6. Same item not reproduced term to term
7. No charge made to students beyond actual photocopy cost

Photocopying of Out-of-Print Material:
(See Chapter 3)

Out of print is not necessarily out of copyright. If copyright still in effect, must request permission.

Off-Air Videotaping for Classroom Use:
(See Chapter 7)

1. Privilege only for nonprofit educational institutions
2. Programs taped must be used directly for instruction and not for entertainment
3. Programs may only be taped from open-air broadcast stations for which no payment is made to receive programs
4. Program taped may be kept 45 calendar days after taping, then must be erased
5. During 45 day period, may only be used with students during first 10 consecutive school days
6. Recordings may only be made at the request of teachers
7. No broadcast program may be recorded off-air more than once for the same teacher, no matter how many times broadcast
8. Limited number of copies may be made to service all teachers requesting use, but all governed by same 10 day use, 45 day erasure period
9. Program must be recorded in its entirety and may not be altered (edited)

Taping From Satellite or Cable for Classroom Use:
(See Chapter 7)

1. Requires permission of the copyright holder
2. Payment of appropriate fees for satellite broadcasts
3. Permissible when copyright holder offers rights without requesting (Ex. Cable in the Classroom programming; C-Span; special satellite broadcasts)
4. May tape programs from cable that may also be received on local, open air broadcast stations (Same channel you can receive with "rabbit ears" is carried on cable")

Utilizing Videotapes With The Home Use Only Warning Label:
(See Chapter 7)

1. Purchased videos may be used for direct instruction only and may not be used for entertainment
2. Rental videos may be used for direct instruction only and may not be used for entertainment. However, if a school or individual signs a membership form or rental agreement limiting the use of the videos to "Home Use Only", this constitutes a contract and the video would not be able to be used in the classroom
3. Libraries may acquire and loan videos
4. Libraries wishing to make videos available for public viewing in the library would need to obtain public performance rights

4

Using Videos On Closed Circuit Systems:
(See Chapter 7)

It would be permissible to show the following types of video programs on a CCTV system **within a single institution**. All programs may only be used for direct instruction, not entertainment.

1. Videos purchased by the educational institution with closed circuit rights
2. Videos for which the copyright holder has granted closed circuit use rights :(Ex. Cable In The Classroom Programming)
3. Videos produced by the institution and not containing copyrighted material (unless permission has been obtained)
4. Simultaneous transmission of live broadcasts
5. In general, most instructional programs purchased from instructional production companies. However, some may charge for closed circuit rights or may permit CCTV use (read literature carefully)
6. In general, most programs provided by state departments of education, higher education governing boards or state library systems. (Check to verify)

The following programs remain questionable as to whether they may be used on closed circuit systems: (Current legal interpretations lean more toward the **not permissible** side)

1. Programs taped off-air under the 10 day use, 45 day erasure guidelines
2. Purchased or rental videos with the "Home Use Only" label

Making Copies of Computer Software:
(See Chapter 8)

By law, the legitimate owner of a legitimate copy of the software may:

1. make a copy or adaptation of the program in order to be able to use the program with the machine
2. make a copy for archival (preservation) purposes (cannot be used as another working copy)

Copying from CD ROM Sources:
(See Chapter 10)

In general, may copy information from CD-ROM periodicals, encyclopedias and other printed works, applying the photocopying guidelines

Copying from the Internet: *(See Chapter 11)*	Unless otherwise stated, one should assume that all materials on the Internet, including web sites, are copyrighted and that existing copyright guidelines apply. When in doubt, permission should be secured from the copyright holder.

Using Copyrighted Material in Multi-Media Productions *(See Chapter 9)*

User Limitations:	1. Students may create, perform and display multimedia productions, for educational uses, only in the course for which it was created and may retain for portfolio use 2. Educators may create, perform and display multimedia productions for educational uses, for the purposes of face-to-face instruction, assigning students to self-study, for remote instruction to students, at peer conferences and may retain for their professional portfolio
Time Limitations:	1. Students may only use their productions for and during the course for which it was prepared. However, they may retain, indefinitely, for their personal portfolio. 2. Educators may use their productions up to two years after the first instructional use with a class. It may be retained indefinitely for portfolio use
Portion Limitations Motion Media:	1. May take up to 10% or 3 minutes, whichever is less, in the aggregate, of a copyrighted motion media work
Portion Limitations Text Material:	1. May take up to 10% or 1,000 words, whichever is less, in the aggregate, from a copyrighted work consisting of text material 2. May use an entire poem of 250 words or less; no more than three poems from one poet or five poems from different poets from an anthology 3. Poems longer than 250 words, may use 250 words, but no more than 3 excerpts by a poet, or 5 excerpts from different poets from a single anthology
Portion Limitations Music, Lyrics, Music Video:	1. May use up to 10% or a maximum of 30 seconds of the music and lyrics from an individual musical work (or in the aggregate of extracts from an individual work)

2. Any alterations to a musical work shall not change the basic melody or the fundamental character of the work

Portion Limitations
Illustrations & Photographs:

1. When using photographs or illustrations from a published collective work, not more than 10% or 15 images, whichever is less, may be used
2. No more than 5 images by an artist or photographer may be used

Portion Limitations
Numerical Data Sets:

1. May take up to 10% or 2500 fields, whichever is less, from a copyrighted database or data table

Copy Limits:

1. Educators may make two use copies of the work they produced, only one of which may be placed on reserve.
2. One additional, preservation copy may be made which may be used to generate replacement copies in the event a use copy is lost, stolen or damaged

Using Copyrighted Materials In Distance Learning
(See Chapter 11)

In general, this requires prior permission from the copyright holder(s) in order to convert from one format to another and to transmit such materials, with exception of the following, TEACH Act privileges.

TEACH Act and Distance Learning

Provides educators and government employees limited privileges in using copyrighted materials, without requiring prior permission.

Activities Permitted:

1. Analog or digital transmissions
2. Delivery of "mediated instruction" within a finite amount of time, comparable to teaching a specific class session.
3. The performance of any form of copyrighted work, but only in "reasonable and limited portions."
4. Displays of copyrighted works comparable to that used in a regular class session, i.e. pictures, photographs, charts, diagrams, sculpture.
5. **Temporary** transmission copies of the copyrighted works may be made. Also permits the conversion of "portions" of works from analog to digital, solely for the purpose of the transmission.

Activities Not Permitted/ Restricted:

1. Converting complete works from analog to digital.
2. Converting videotapes or other analog sources to digital

format for the purpose of video streaming or to set up on demand video servers, when the purpose and use of the materials would extend beyond the time of a normal, class period or session.

3. Transmission restricted to students/government employees enrolled in course.
4. All performances and displays must be at the direction or under direct supervision of the teacher/instructor.
5. Copyrighted material transmitted must be an integral part of the class session and not supplemental or an enhancement.
6. Copyrighted works marketed for use specifically in distance learning may not be used under the TEACH Act. Use would be governed by contract or license agreement.
7. Performance and displays may only be made from copies lawfully made or acquired.

Copyright Office Address Telephone Numbers and Web Site:

1. Copyright Office, Library of Congress, Washington, DC, 20559-6000
2. To speak to an information specialist, M-F, 8:30-5:00, call 202-707-3000 (They do not interpret the law)
3. To request publications or applications forms, 24hrs/day, call 202-707-9100
4. Web site: http://lcweb.loc.gov/copyright/

©Corel Gallery

Chapter 1 - Items Protected/ Not Protected

What is Copyright?

Copyright is a form of protection, provided by Title 17, U.S. Code, to the authors of "original works of authorship". This protection is available for both published and unpublished works.

The basis of the copyright law of the United States can be found in the Constitution[1] where Congress was granted the power "to promote the Progress of Science and useful Arts, by securing for limited Times to Authors and Inventors the exclusive Right to their respective Writings and Discoveries." The law was written in such a manner as to both acknowledge the rights of authors and the rights of society to information. As a result, the copyright law offers authors protection for their creative efforts for a limited period of time, after which the material enters the public domain and is accessible by everyone.

What Is Protected Under Copyright?

Copyright protection is granted for "original works of authorship" when they become fixed in a tangible form of expression, such as the written word, a picture, an audiovisual program, etc. The fixing in a tangible form doesn't have to be directly perceptible, as long as it may be communicated with the aid of a machine or device, i.e. a videocassette recorder, DVD player, etc.

There are currently eight categories of works that are eligible for copyright protection. They are:

1. literary works
2. musical works, including any accompanying words
3. dramatic works, including any accompanying music
4. pantomimes and choreographic works
5. pictorial, graphic and sculptural works
6. motion pictures and other audiovisual works
7. sound recordings
8. architectural works

The preceding categories should be viewed in the broadest sense. As examples, computer programs, which are actually sets of directions telling computers what to do, are registered as literary works. Maps and architectural plans are registered as pictorial, graphic and sculptural works. Videocassettes are categorized as motion pictures and other audiovisual works.

What Is Not Protected Under Copyright?

In general, copyright doesn't protect ideas, but rather the form or format in which the ideas are expressed. The following categories are generally **not** eligible for copyright protection:

- Ideas, procedures, methods, systems, processes, concepts, principles, discoveries, or devices, as distinguished from a description, explanation, or illustration.

> **Note:** *Even though not protected by copyright, Patent Law does apply to ideas, processes, and inventions. Authors are granted protection for 17 years, non-renewable.*

- Works that are not fixed in a tangible form of expression such as choreographic works that have not been notated or recorded, or improvisational speeches or performances that have not been written or recorded.

- Titles, names, short phrases and slogans, familiar symbols or designs, mere variations in typographic ornamentation, lettering or coloring. The mere listing of ingredients or contents is normally not copyrightable, unless accompanied by substantial explanation or direction or in the case of compiling a number of recipes together.

> **Note:** *Symbols, designs or names used to identify a person's goods or services so as to distinguish them from the goods and services produced by others are protected under Trademark Law. Holders of a Trademark may renew indefinitely in 10 year cycles. The letters **TM** or **R** by themselves, or in a circle, often denote such protection.* ***Example:*** *Pepsi-Cola and Coca-Cola are trademarked names.*

- Works consisting entirely of information that is common property and containing no original authorship. **Examples:** Standard calendars; height and weight charts; tape measures and rules; lists or tables taken from public documents or other common sources; blank forms such as time cards, graph paper, account books, diaries, address books, and order forms designed to record, rather than convey, information.

Chapter 2 - Fair Use

As indicated in the introduction, the Copyright Law attempts to balance the protection of the rights of the author with the needs of society. Even though the author or creator is given certain specific rights under Section 106 of the law, Section 107 begins to set some limitations on those rights followed, in other sections, by specific exemptions granted for particular situations.

Criteria & Guidelines

The courts use the following four criteria to determine Fair Use:

A. The purpose and character of the use, including whether the use is of a commercial nature or is for nonprofit educational purposes.

The Preamble to Section 107 lists the following purposes as considerations for Fair Use:

1. Criticism, comment and news reporting
2. Teaching, scholarship or research

However, even when the use falls within the preceding areas, it does not require that the courts declare "Fair Use", since "Fair Use" presupposes good faith and fair dealing.

B. The nature of the copyrighted work.

1. Materials designed primarily for educational use, i.e. textbooks and periodicals for students, are less susceptible to a claim of Fair Use than a general circulation item, such as a popular magazine.
2. The claim for Fair Use is greater in the case of factual works than for creative, original or fiction works.
3. Works that are more an act of diligence or compilation rather than originality ie. a catalog, index, directory, are more open to a claim of Fair Use.
4. If a work is determined to be of an entertainment nature, it is less likely to a claim of Fair Use.

C. The amount and substantiality (extent) of the portion used in relationship to the copyrighted work as a whole.

This is considered both in terms of quantity and quality of what was reproduced. In general, if the entire work was reproduced, a claim cannot be made for Fair Use.

D. The effect of the use upon the potential market for or value of the copyrighted work.

   1. This is judged not only if the material is in the same medium, but also if it is in another medium. (Example: A book is narrated onto audiotape. The fact that the company currently produces the work only in print form doesn't prevent a suit based upon the effect on future sales if the material was to later be made available on tape. The courts consider future use in another medium affecting the author's protection of the creation of a derivative work.)

   2. The courts also view this section not just in terms of the specific case, but "what if" Fair Use is granted in this instance, what would happen if others performed the same act.

The Functional Test

The four Fair Use criteria outlined above must all be met in order for the courts to award a judgment of Fair Use. To further assist in the determination, the functional test is applied:

> If the material reproduced, performed, displayed, etc. serves the same function as the original material, it is not subject to Fair Use. i.e. reproducing lyrics from sheet music to make up a song sheet.

Satire, Burlesque and Parody

These areas are generally regarded as Fair Use if meeting the four fair use criteria and as long as a "substantial portion of the original material is not used."[1]

Incidental Reproduction

Several court cases have indicated that while filming a scene, if a copyrighted item, such as the cover of a magazine or the performance of copyrighted music is picked up incidentally to the production, i.e. live coverage of a parade, that the incidental copying of copyrighted material would be considered Fair Use.[2] Fair Use would not apply to the willful inclusion of such material.

Other Fair Use Applications

In general, students, to meet requirements and to demonstrate competency in a class, may utilize copyrighted material for the creation of a presentation or for the purpose of analysis and criticism. Short exercises, such as copying a brief segment from a work while learning to touch type would, in most instances, be considered Fair Use, as long as extensive sections of a work were not utilized and the copies of materials produced were not retained or duplicated.

In the following sections of this guide, other exceptions, exemptions and special Fair Use applications are listed under appropriate headings that make it somewhat easier for educators, librarians and media staff to find information appropriate to their areas of interest and concern.

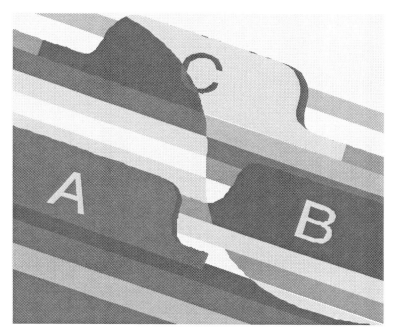

© Microsoft Clip Art

Chapter 3 - Photocopying

The following Fair Use guidelines for classroom and teacher photocopying was the result of activity by a committee of authors, publishers and educators who made their recommendations to Congress. The guidelines were endorsed by the House in the House Report.[i]

Teacher/Classroom Photocopying

You May Reproduce Single Copies of the Following:

©Microsoft Clip Art

1. A chapter of a book

2. An article from a periodical or newspaper

3. A short story, short essay or short poem, whether or not from a collective work

4. A chart, graph, diagram,*cartoon or picture from a book, periodical or newspaper

Intent of the preceding: For scholarly research, teaching or preparation to teach a class.

   ***Note:** Copyrighted, syndicated cartoon characters are not permitted to be copied.*

You May Reproduce Multiple Copies of the Following:

1. A complete poem if less than 250 words and if printed on not more than two pages

2. An excerpt from a long poem, but not to exceed 250 words

3. A complete article, story or essay of less than 2,500 words or an excerpt, not more than 1000 words, from a larger printed work not to exceed 10% of the whole, whichever of the preceding is less

4. One chart, graph, diagram,*cartoon or picture per book or periodical issue

   This is a minimum. Maximum is not stated. Concept is to take a very small portion from a work and the part taken is not the most creative essence of the work.

5. Special works combining prose, poetry and illustrations, but limited to no more than 10% of the total

   This is further clarified in the House Report where it is stated that " certain works in

poetry prose or in "poetic prose" which often combine language with illustrations and which are intended for children and at other times for a more general audience fall short of 2500 words in their entirety. These special works may not be reproduced in their entirety; however, an excerpt comprising not more than two of the published pages of such a special work and containing not more than 10% of the words found in the text thereof, may be reproduced."

6. All preceding must bear the copyright notice

Limits to the Preceding:

1. Copying is made for one course only

2. One work from a single author

3. No more than three authors from a collective work

4. No more than 9 instances of such multiple copying in one class term

5. Copying shall not be used to create or replace or substitute for anthologies or collective works

6. Copying of "consumable" works i.e.. workbooks, exercises, standardized tests, test booklets and answer sheets is absolutely prohibited

7. Same item not reproduced term to term

8. No charge made to students beyond actual photocopying

*Note: The limitations stated above **do not** apply to current news periodicals, newspapers and current news sections of other periodicals. Multiple copies of these items may be made for classroom use as long as they are not reproduced from sources designed specifically for student use, i.e.. Scholastic Magazine.*

Library Photocopying

©IMSI

(Copies & Phonorecords) - Exempt Conditions[2]

1. Reproduction of unpublished works for the purpose of preservation and security

    a. Up to three copies or phonorecords may be made
    b. Item being reproduced must currently be in the collections of the library/archive

    c. Any copy or phonorecord reproduced in digital format may only be made available to the public on the premises of the library/archives

2. Reproduction of published works for the purpose of replacement of damaged, deteriorating, lost or stolen copies or if the existing format in which the work is stored has become obsolete

    a. If an unused replacement cannot be obtained at a fair price
    b. Up to three copies or phonorecords may be made
    c. Any copy or phonorecord reproduced in digital format is not made available to the public, in that format, outside of the premises of the library/archives that is in lawful possession of such a copy

3. Reproduction for a patron of 1 single copy of one article or small part of a work to become the property of the patron for the purpose of study or research. Copyright warning notice (**see Appendix B**) must be displayed at the desk where orders for copies are accepted or placed in view near a walk-up copy station

4. Reproduction of an entire work, at the request of a patron, if it cannot be obtained at a fair price

    a. Copy becomes the property of the patron

    b. Copyright warning notice (**see Appendix B**) must be displayed at the desk where orders for copies are accepted or placed in view near a walk-up copy station

Libraries are not liable for wrongful copying done on public machines if they have placed copyright warning notices on machines.

Systematic Reproduction

NOTE: All of the preceding are for isolated and unrelated reproduction on different occasions. *Systematic, single reproduction is prohibited.*

Libraries and library employees are given notice in Section 108 (g)(1) that the rights of reproduction do not extend to "multiple copying of the same material on one occasion or over a period of time, and intended for aggregate use by one or more individuals or for the separate use by individual members of a group. The library has the right to refuse to reproduce materials under the belief that the request is related to a concerted or planned effort to reproduce or produce in the aggregate.

Following are examples of systematic reproduction which are <u>not</u> considered to be Fair Use or permissible.

1. An instructor assigns a research paper and requires all students to use the same resources and to copy the same material.

2. A library with a specialized collection of journals notifies other libraries that it will make copies of articles for them. As a result, the requesting libraries discontinue or refrain from purchasing these journals.

3. A research center subscribes to one or more copies of periodicals and makes available copies of articles to all staff who request them. By making the articles available in this manner, it is in lieu of multiple subscriptions.

4. One branch of a library system subscribes to a journal and makes copies for users at other branches, in lieu of the other branches having their own subscriptions.

5. Central Source Libraries, whose principal purpose is to provide copies to others, supply systematically. Therefore, they are not qualified for the library photocopying exemption.

Rights Of Reproduction Do Not Apply To:

1. Musical works

2. Pictorial, graphic or sculptural works

3. Motion picture or other audiovisual works (Exception: Motion picture or videotape of a news program)

Library Photocopying for Reserve Use

The Copyright Law did not specifically address copying for reserve use. However, the law still governs the making of photocopies. Library photocopying for reserve use may be permissible if all of the four Section 107 Fair Use criteria, detailed earlier in this guide, are met.

* Purpose and Character of Use
* Nature of the Work
* Amount and substantiality of the portion used
* Effect upon the potential market for the work

Libraries that carefully examine their reserve requests, monitor the volume of reproduction, keep the quantities of copies to a minimum, and only reproduce small sections of a total work will probably fall under the category of Fair Use. When feasible, prior copyright permission from the source would help to solidify one's legal position.[3] If the reserve material is to be used term-to-term, permission from the copyright holder would be required.

This doesn't negate the Section 108 guidelines for library photocopying whereby individual requests for copies of material for scholarly research may be made, as long they become the property of the user.

However, systematic single copying of materials placed on reserve would not be permissible. Libraries placing materials on reserve will be held responsible for monitoring the reproduction of such materials by patrons.

Library Photocopying for Interlibrary Loan

Section 108(g)(2) of the Copyright Law addressed the subject of interlibrary loan with a key proviso that the loan arrangements do not have as their purpose or effect "that the libraries or archives receiving such copies or phonorecords for distribution does so in such aggregate quantities as to substitute for a subscription to or purchase of such a work." The question then arose as to what would be considered aggregate quantities and what would be the condition under which interlibrary loan crossed the line into illegal copying in substitution for the purchase of the material.

To respond to this need, The National Commission on New Technological Uses of Copyrighted Works, a commission charged by Congress and representing principal library, author and publisher organizations, agreed to the following detailed guidelines, which were accepted into the Conference Report of the 94th Congress.[4]

1. Within any calendar year, a requesting library may not request more than five copies of any article or articles published in a given periodical during the five years prior to to the date of requesting reproduction. This guideline applies even if the copies were of different articles from separate issues of the periodical. This limit does not apply to articles published prior to this five-year period, but leaves open the question as to whether this would indicate an "open door" for requests.

   Clarification: A library is limited to a total of five copies from a periodical for the prior five-year period. Therefore, if a request was placed, in 2002, for a copy of five separate articles from a single edition of a periodical, no further requests could be made for copies from the same or any other edition of that same named periodical that had been published during the period of 1998-2002.

2. Within any calendar year, a requesting library is limited to requesting no more than five copies of materials, other than an article, in any given work. This limitation applies to reproduction of and from materials that are not periodicals and also to materials from periodicals not considered articles, such as prose, poetry and fiction. This limit is for the entire period that the material is covered by copyright, not just the preceding five years.

3. If the library requesting an interlibrary loan already subscribes to the same periodical or has ordered the periodical or owns a copy of the source from which they are requesting the copy, they are not restricted by the two preceding guidelines. Instead, this type of copy request is treated as though the requesting entity was copying from its own collection under the regular Library Photocopying Guidelines. CONTU, in making this recommendation, recognized that there might be instances where even though an institution owned the material, it might not have been readily available for duplication.

4. No request for a copy or phonorecord of any material to which these guidelines apply may be fulfilled by the supplying entity unless such request is accompanied by a representation by the requesting entity that the request was made in conformity with these guidelines.

5. The requesting library shall maintain records of all requests made by it for copies or phonorecords of any materials to which these guidelines apply and shall maintain records of the fulfillment of such requests. These records shall be retained until the end of the third complete calendar year after the end of the calendar year in which the respective request shall have been made.

Photocopying of Out-of-Print Materials

The fact that an item is no longer in print or available does not negate the copyright protection for the author that exists with the material. An institution, library or an individual may not automatically proceed to making copies of out of print materials.

A reasonable investigation should take place to establish who is the current copyright holder of the material and to seek permission to reproduce. This search should utilize commonly known trade sources to identify the copyright holder, if this is not clearly identified on the publication page of the work. Keep copies of all correspondence and return envelopes to document that an attempt has been made to pursue copyright permission. Further protection, prior to duplicating materials, may be gained by pursuing information as to the current copyright holder of the material by requesting that a search take place. This may be instituted, for a fee, by a request directed to:

> Reference and Bibliography Section
> LM-451
> Copyright Office, Library of Congress
> Washington, D.C. 20559
> (202) 707-6850

Additional sources for searches and for obtaining copyright permissions may be found in Chapter 12 of this guide, entitled **Obtaining Copyright Permission**.

Facsimile Reproduction (Fax Copying)

A facsimile or FAX machine is a copy machine and is subject to the same copyright considerations as any other copier. The same rules of classroom, library photocopying and interlibrary loan apply.

The necessity of making a photocopy of the material in order to utilize the fax machine is not a violation as long as the photocopy is destroyed after transmission. The fax copy, as received on the transmission end, now constitutes the only legal copy. As with all photocopying for interlibrary loan, the copy should bear the copyright warning notice. It is recommended that the same copyright warning notice posted near copy machines be posted near the fax machine.

Fair Use Questions/Situations

Making "Big Books"

At several conferences, vendors have made presentations about how elementary students can become involved in using materials taken or copied from books to create "big books." Does the copyright law permit such an activity to take place?

No, there is no provision for permitting anyone to create a derivative work, unless the author grants such permission. What has added to the confusion is that there are some firms who are selling materials for which they hold the copyright and are granting permission for schools to use these materials to encourage teachers and students to create " big books." However, some individuals have generalized this type of permission so as to apply to all copyrighted sources and that is not the case. Once again, since the copyright holder is given a set of rights when they copyright their material, they may also give or sell those rights away. However, this would be on an individual, case-by-case basis, and cannot be generalized from one or two companies providing such permission.

Sharing Resources Via Fax

Would the use of fax machines, in various branches of a library system or educational institution's media/learning resource centers, in order to be able to share resources, such as articles from periodicals, be considered legal?

Under certain circumstances, this may be permissible. Fax copies are treated as though they are photocopies and follow the photocopying guidelines. It would be permissible to transmit materials, such as periodical articles, between library facilities for the purpose of interlibrary loan. However, this type of copying is limited to no more than five copies of articles from a single magazine title over a five-year period. The intent is to provide interlibrary loan, but not in lieu of the purchase of subscriptions as a result of producing sufficient copies that would negate the need to purchase subscriptions. The use of a fax machine in order to reduce the purchase of subscriptions on the basis that the institution views itself as one entity, rather than as separate branch libraries, is not considered legal.

Presenters Copying and Distributing Articles

Are presenters, at conferences and meetings, permitted to make copies of copyrighted articles, according to photocopying guidelines, and distribute them to those in attendance?

Without prior permission, this activity is not permissible. The reference to making multiple copies, under the photocopying guidelines, specifically pertains to classroom use when the time for writing for permission would limit the ability to use these materials with a class. Since the materials, in this situation, are not being used for classroom instruction and there is more than sufficient time to write for permission, this distribution would not fall under fair use. However, it would be perfectly legal to distribute a bibliography of suggested readings.

It is also important to remember that unless one obtains permission, in writing, from the copyright holder, to copy the materials and to extend that right to the audience, that the only permission normally given is for the presenter to duplicate and distribute in that one, specific time/location. Many times, attendees at conferences pick up copies of materials that are copyrighted and believe if they were handed out in quantity, that they may go back to their institutions and reproduce the materials for their own needs. Therefore, it is suggested that a statement be made to attendees indicating if the material being handed out may or may not be reproduced.

Black-line Master Books

A black-line master book is purchased at the request of a fifth grade teacher. May all of the teachers of fifth grade in that school utilize the master book for their classes?

Black-line master books are generally sold with the right to indefinitely reproduce materials for the "teacher's classroom." In general, they are not sold with the right to reproduce for more than the one teacher. If such rights are desired, they should be negotiated with the copyright holder prior to purchase or a clarification made as to the actual duplication rights given the school at the time of purchase.

Reproducing Out-of-Print Materials

A paperback literature work is no longer in print. May the teacher reproduce the work for use in her class?

Out-of-print does not necessarily mean "out-of-copyright." As long as the work is still under copyright protection, one could not go ahead and reproduce without obtaining prior permission.

Reprinting Current News Articles for Classroom Use

May an instructor reprint a current news article from the local newspaper to distribute to his classes for the purpose of discussion?

It is permissible to make classroom quantity copies of current news articles for instructional purposes, as long as the individual article is not copyrighted and is not taken from a source designed specifically for the educational market, i.e. Scholastic Magazine.

Chapter 4 - Public Performance

Section 106(4) of the Copyright Act provides that in the case of literary, musical, dramatic and choreographic works, pantomimes, motion pictures and other audiovisual works, the copyright owner has the exclusive right to perform the work publicly. To perform a work means "to recite, render, play, dance, or act it, either directly or by means of any device or process..."[1] A work is performed publicly if it is performed "at a place open to the public or at any place where a substantial number of persons outside of a normal circle of a family and its social acquaintances is gathered..."[2]

With the preceding information, one would assume that libraries and educational institutions would be prohibited from performing such works. However, the following exemptions pertain to these areas. **(Also see Chapters 5, 6 and 7)**

Public Performance In A Classroom

Section 110(1) of the Copyright Law provides a special performance privilege (exemption) for educators. It allows the performance of those works defined in Section 106(4) subject to the following conditions and limitations:[3]

1. The performance is allowed only for face-to-face teaching activities directly related to instruction. This was intended to exclude outside transmissions i.e. radio and television, whether open broadcast or closed circuit.[4]

2. However, "as long as the instructor and pupils are in the same building or general area, the exemption would extend to the use of devices for amplifying sounds and for projecting images."[5] Thus "face-to-face" does not require that the teacher and students be able to see each other, although it does require their simultaneous presence in the same general place."[6]

3. The exemption only applies to non-profit educational institutions.

4. Performances of the defined works must only be by the instructor or pupils. However, the House Report included guest lecturers if their instructional activities were confined to the classroom activities.

5. Exemption only applies to performances related to teaching activities which involve systematic instruction. Performances for recreation or intellectual appeal and not related to specific teaching activities are not eligible for the exemption. **(See Bibliography, Licens-**

ing/Performance Rights for Sources of Videos with Public Performance Rights)

6. The performance must take place in a classroom or similar place devoted to instruction. Such other places would include studios, workshops, training fields, a library, the stage of an auditorium, a training field, or gym if they are being used for systematic, instructional activity.

7. The exemption would not apply to "performances in an auditorium or stadium during a school assembly, graduation ceremony, class play, or sporting event, where the audience is not confined to the members of a particular class."[7] Therefore, to avoid misinterpretation, Section 110(1) of the Copyright Act is an exemption for classroom, not school performances.

All of the preceding limitations related to this exemption apply when the institution has desired to perform an appropriate work in the classroom. However, the right of performance via closed circuit television or to perform in an auditorium may be negotiated at the time of purchase of the particular program or the performance right may be licensed by negotiating such an agreement. The law doesn't prevent the copyright holder from giving his/her rights to the institution, if the copyright owner agrees to such a performance. Therefore, one may always write for permission even if a specific performance exemption doesn't exist.

Public Performance In A Library

In the most technical sense, libraries are subject to the performance restrictions of the copyright law. There are no specific exemptions in the performance area as there are for photocopying. Libraries, by their nature, constitute a site where the public gathers and as a result, any performance would be considered a public performance. Single viewing would, in the aggregate, be multiple viewing of any copyrighted program. However, by past practice, it has come to be accepted when a patron listens to an audio recording, or views a film or video in a carrel or booth. In terms of the video format, however, this medium is in question as to whether it can be drawn into the past precedent set by the other performances that have been tacitly accepted over the years. A court decision in the commercial sector, the Redd Horne case, brings its use in libraries into question, especially related to the use of videocassettes designed for home use.

In the case of educational libraries, the classroom performance exemption would apply if the activity taking place is directly related to instruction. Such an example would be the teaching of media skills using a videotape or DVD. It would also appear that students required to view a video as part of a classroom activity directly related to their instruction, not simply to stimulate interest, would be able to do so in the library. However, if the library simply makes materials available for casual browsing and viewing, they would not be operating under the classroom, instructional exemption and would be in violation of the performance right of the author/producer.

Libraries may acquire the rights for performance at the time of purchase of the material or may negotiate licenses or request permission after owning the material. In the case of educational institutions, the majority of software vendors sell the material with the knowledge and permission that it will be used in the library or media center when it is purchased by that center or library. As a general guideline, all libraries, for self-protection, should verify their performance rights at the time of purchase. There is no problem in loaning materials to patrons for their use. **(See Bibliography for Licensing/Performance Rights/Non-Instructional Video Performances)**

Public Performance At School Assemblies

There is no specific exemption for public performances in schools for other than the classroom/ instructional applications. However, the exemption for Nonprofit Performances[8] would apply to educational institutions and libraries as well. The following conditions and limitations apply to this area.

1. Limited solely to performances of non-dramatic literary and musical works.

2. Performance given directly in the presence of the audience.

3. Performance given without any purpose of direct or indirect commercial advantage.

4. Compensation for promoters, performers or organizers is prohibited. However, others connected with the performance, such as sound and lighting technicians, ushers, etc. may be paid. In addition, as in the case of a salaried music teacher conducting an orchestra as part of his/her assigned responsibility, the exemption would still apply.

5. A direct or indirect admission charge may not be made, with the following exception:

    The net proceeds are used for educational, religious or charitable purposes.

    The copyright holder has the right to oppose the admission charge with seven days notice prior to the date of the performance. However, there is no requirement to notify the copyright holder in advance of the performance.

Performance By Non-profit Veterans or Fraternal Organizations

Section 110(10) of the law provides a performance exemption under the following conditions:

1. When a non-dramatic literary or musical work is performed.
2. When the work performed is used for a social function.
3. When the general public is not invited.
4. When the proceeds are used exclusively for charitable purposes.

It should be noted that these exemptions do not apply to college or university fraternities or sororities unless the social function is being held solely to raise funds for charitable purposes.

Chapter 5 - Music

The following guidelines were developed by a committee representing educators, publishers and producers and incorporated into the House Report of the 94th Congress. They have been accepted as the intent of the Fair Use (Section 107) of the Copyright Act as pertains to the educational uses of music.[1] Italicized information in each section has been added to provide clarification and examples, but is not part of the House Report.

As guidelines, the following establishes the minimum and not the maximum standards of educational fair use. Fair use is always open to interpretation and even the courts weigh each case on individual merits. However, the guidelines establish the "safe harbor" approach.

Permissible Uses

1. Emergency copying to replace purchased copies which, for any reason, are not available for an imminent performance provided purchased replacement copies shall be substituted in due course.

2. a. * For academic purposes, other than performance, single or multiple copies of excerpts of works may be made, provided the excerpts do not comprise a part of the whole which would constitute a performable unit such as a section, movement or aria, but in no case more than 10% of the whole work. The number of copies shall not exceed one copy per pupil. (* *The wording of this paragraph was corrected in 122 Congressional Record House 10875, September 22, 1976*)

    b. For academic purposes, other than performance, a single copy of an entire performable unit (section, movement, aria, etc.) that is, (1) confirmed by the copyright proprietor to be out of print or (2) unavailable except in a larger work, may be made by or for a teacher solely for the purpose of his or her scholarly research or in preparation to teach a class.

3. Printed copies, which have been purchased, may be edited or simplified provided that the fundamental character of the work is not distorted or the lyrics, if any, altered or lyrics added if none exist.

4. A single copy of recordings of performances by students may be made for evaluation or rehearsal purposes and may be retained by the educational institution or individual teacher.

5. A single copy of a sound recording (such as a tape, disc or cassette) of copyrighted music may be made from sound recordings owned by an educational institution or an individual teacher for the purpose of constructing aural exercises or examinations and may be

retained by the educational institution or individual teacher. (This pertains only to the copyright of the music itself and not to any copyright which may exist in the sound recording.

However, this does not permit the creation of a recording for teaching purposes other than constructing aural exercises or testing.

Prohibitions

1. Copying to create or replace or substitute for anthologies, compilations or collective works.

2. Copying of or from works intended to be "consumable" in the course of study or of teaching such as workbooks, exercises, standardized tests and answer sheets and like material.

3. Copying for the purpose of a performance, except as noted under Permissible Uses.

   It is not permissible to make copies in order to provide extra parts for one instrument. Nor is it permissible to make copies for contests or for choral or speaking parts for musical plays. Additional copies need to be purchased or duplication rights negotiated.

4. Copying for the purpose of substituting for the purchase of music, except as noted under Permissible Uses.

5. Copying without inclusion of the copyright notice, which appears on the printed copy.

Other Considerations

1. Recording of a band or concert and selling copies is not considered Fair Use. Any recordings made of bands, show choirs, choirs, etc. require payment of a mechanical royalty, even if used as a fund raiser and not for profit. The Harry Fox agency (**see Bibliography**) acts as an agency to handle such rights and royalty payments. A request may be made to record for the purpose of a fund raiser.

2. Festival organizers or organizations sponsoring a music festival are responsible for making the mechanical royalty payments for any recordings that are made of copyrighted music.

3. Any arrangement of a copyrighted musical work, without the permission of the copyright owner, is considered a copyright infringement. This falls into the category of creating a derivative work, one of the five rights granted an author. Examples of derivative type works in music are arrangements, transcriptions, adaptations, translations of texts, orchestrations, instrumental accompaniments to vocal publications and parody lyrics.

(An example of parody lyrics would be that a show choir has written words to *God Bless America* and intends to perform this at a graduation ceremony. Permission would first have to be obtained from the copyright holder)[2]

4. You may edit or simplify printed copies (of music) which have been purchased, but in no case may one write a derivation or arrangement of a copyrighted work and then photocopy (reproduce) it for classroom use. A copyrighted work must not be distorted or altered without written permission of the copyright owner.

Also See:

Public Performances of Music - Chapter 4
Educational Multimedia - Chapter 9
The Internet and Distance Learning - Chapter 11

©Microsoft Clip Art

Fair Use Questions/Situations

Reproducing Sheet Music for Extra Sections

1. May a music teacher reproduce three extra flute sections from purchased sheet music because she is short copies in this year's class?

   This would be a violation of copyright, since this is not one of the exemptions that permit the reproduction of sheet music. It also does not meet the fair use criteria in that it affects the income of the copyright holder and has, as its purpose, the avoidance of the purchase of additional copies of the music.

Reproducing Sheet Music for a Performance

2. May a music teacher reproduce sheet music for a performance for which he has ordered the appropriate material, but it has not arrived in time?

   This is permissible. However, once the ordered music has arrived, the temporary copies must be destroyed.

Chapter 6 - Audiovisual Works

These unofficial guidelines, based upon Fair Use criteria, legal opinions, court cases and the suggestions of producers and educators, have been in effect since 1976 and have been accepted in practice, although there is no specific section of the law pertaining to this area. However, guidelines do exist for using portions of copyrighted works in the production of multi-media presentations, as well as for use in distance learning. **(See Chapter 9, Educational Multimedia and Chapter 11, Internet and Distance Learning)**

Permissible Uses

1. Creating a series of slides or overhead transparencies from multiple sources, such as magazines, books, encyclopedias, etc., as long as one doesn't exceed one photograph, drawing, chart or diagram per source.

2. Creating a single overhead transparency from a single page of a consumable workbook, not exceeding the one page from the entire book.

3. Salvaging useful frames from a damaged filmstrip in order to create a slide set, as long the slides are maintained in the same chronological order as the original filmstrip, minus the damaged frames.

4. Using an opaque projector to enlarge a map of an area for tracing in a larger scale, as long as the map is not reproduced with those parts that make it copyrightable i.e. color scheme, shading, how cities, buildings are symbolized, etc.

5. Duplicating visual or audio materials from a non-dramatic literary work in order to provide materials for the deaf or the blind. In addition, these and other copyrighted materials may be legally transmitted to blind or deaf individuals via cable or closed circuit systems.

Prohibitions

©Microsoft Clip Art

1. No duplication of audiocassette tapes for archival, backup, or for multiple uses unless reproduction rights were given at the time of purchase.

*2. No reproduction of musical works (i.e. records, tapes, CD's) or conversion from one form to another, such as a record to a tape, unless such rights have been acquired from the copyright holder.

3. No reproduction of any audiovisual work in its entirety, except for off-air video taping as per the guidelines found in the Video section of this guide.

4. No conversion of one media format to another, i.e. 16m.m. film to videotape, with the exception(s) that (1) copies of old motion picture films, subject to deterioration, (mainly pre-1942) may be made for archival preservation and (2) libraries may convert media formats that are no longer in production and for which the equipment to playback or perform is no longer in production (3) are provided by the TEACH Act for distance learning. (See Chapter 11, Internet and Distance Learning)

5. No narrating entire stories onto audio tape.

*NOTE: Protection under copyright is only for sounds as they exist. This doesn't prevent a performance or recording in which sounds are imitated. Infringement occurs when all or a substantial portion of the actual sounds are reproduced. Mere imitation doesn't constitute copyright infringement.

Fair Use Questions/Situations

Reading Stories Onto Tape/CD

Teachers would like to be able to read stories onto tapes or CD's that could then be taken home by students and would support the reading program in the school. The stories would be taken from library books. Is there any problem with making these recordings?

One of the rights granted an author is the sole right to create a derivative work based upon their original work. In this instance, the audiotape would be such a derivative work. Copyright basically protects the format in which an author expresses an idea. (Ideas themselves are not protected) However, don't hesitate to write to the copyright holders of the materials desired to be used, since they may grant permission for taping if you are specific as to the reasons for wanting to change format and indicating the quantity of such tapes that might be produced.

It should also be noted that there is one exemption in the law that would permit the recording of stories. That would be in the instance where the materials were being provided to students who have been identified as legally blind.

Copying/Reproducing Photographs

©Microsoft Clip Art

May a social studies teacher utilize a book containing a number of photographs of the Parthenon in Greece for the purpose of copying several pictures from the book to make a class presentation on architecture?

Copyright law guidelines provide, as a minimum for fair use, the making of one copy of a diagram, chart or picture from a single source. Since the instructor is desirous of copying more than one photograph from the source, copyright permission should be pursued. However, if the instructor is producing a multimedia presentation or desiring to use multiple images in a distance learning environment, limited permission does exist. (See Chapters 9 and 11)

Tracing Cartoon Characters

May a teacher trace the cartoon character "Snoopy" then copy and hand out to students in order to provide interest and motivation for a reading exercise?

The reproduction, in any form, of copyrighted cartoon characters is prohibited.

Converting Records to Tape or CD's

Is it legal to copy an institutionally owned record, that is part of our library collection, onto a cassette tape or CD? We are no longer are using record players.

Libraries have a privilege, under the law, to make up to three copies of materials that are deteriorating for preservation purposes. This conversion of format cannot legally be done simply for the convenience of using a cassette or CD, but to preserve a deteriorating copy. The Digital Millennium Act has further given libraries the privilege of making copies when the format is no longer in manufacture and the equipment to playback is no longer available. These privileges are solely for libraries. One cannot perform such activities for classroom collections of materials or for materials purchased for classroom use, but not part of the library collection.

Chapter 7 - Video

Off-air Videotaping

Institutional Taping

©IMSI

In terms of off-air videotaping for educational use, there exists a set of Fair Use guidelines that were never adopted into law, but have tacitly become accepted as the "official" guideline for education. They were developed by a subcommittee of Congress, chaired by Representative Kastenmeir, which was attempting to deal with the problem of providing legitimate access to programs for instructional use. According to these guidelines, an educational institution may tape programs off-air if they adhere to the following conditions:[1] *(Italicized information in each section has been added to provide clarification and examples, but are not part of the guidelines)*

1. The privilege of off-air taping applies only to non-profit, educational institutions.

    Programs taped must be used directly for instruction and not for entertainment.

2. A broadcast program may be recorded off-air simultaneously with broadcast transmission (including cable transmission) and retained by the educational institution for a period not to exceed (45) calendar days after the date of recording. The program then must be erased.

    "Broadcast programs" are defined as those programs transmitted by television stations without charge to the general public. Only those cable programs available on-air (open broadcast) in your area may be taped. As an example, if you receive and NBC station locally with a regular antenna, that is open broadcast. If the reception is better on cable, you could tape the NBC station from cable. However, pay services such as out-of-town stations, HBO and Cinemax do not fall under these guidelines.

    However, there are some parts of the country in which there are no on-air services available and reception is provided solely by cable or satellite. In the Senate Committee Report [2], prior to the adoption of the off- air taping guidelines, in providing examples of Fair Use related to "other situations", " the committee's attention has been directed to the special problems involved in the reception of instructional television programs in remote areas of the country. The committee believes that the making by a school located in such a remote area of an off-the-air recording of an instructional television transmission for the purpose of delayed viewing of the program by students for the same school constitutes Fair Use." It would appear that minimally, remote schools could tape, from cable or satellite, programs of an instructional nature, such as those from PBS. However, taping of non-instructional programming from other commercial stations is not clear. Such rights may often be obtained from the cable or satellite companies providing such services to remote areas. Once again, however, pay services such as bringing in stations very distant from your geographical location, HBO, and Cinemax would not fall under this interpretation.

3. Even though the programs may be held (45) days, they may only be used once and repeated once with each class by an individual teacher during the first ten (10) consecutive school days during the forty-five (45) day calendar retention period. They may not be used with students after that time. *School days do not include weekends, holidays, vacations, examination periods or other scheduled interruptions.*

4. After the first ten (10) consecutive school days, off-air recordings may be used up to the end of the (45) day retention period only for teacher evaluation purposes and may not be used for student exhibition or any other non-evaluation purpose without authorization.

5. Off-air recordings may be made only at the request of and used by individual teachers, and may not be regularly recorded in anticipation of requests. *(Automatic recording by a media specialist)* No broadcast program may be recorded off-air more than once at the request of the same teacher, regardless of the number of times the program may be broadcast.

6. A limited number of copies may be reproduced from each off-air recording to meet the legitimate needs of teachers under these guidelines. *(To meet the requests of several teachers for the same program)* Each additional copy shall be subject to all provisions governing the original recording.

7. The program must be recorded in its entirety, including copyright notice, and may not be altered.* Off-air recordings may not be physically or electronically combined or merged to constitute teaching anthologies or compilations. *Note: However, during playback, sections may be omitted that are not felt to be appropriate. Programs need not be used in their entirety.*

   *Deaf & Hearing Impaired -A Fair Use interpretation, by House Copyright Committee Chairperson, Robert W.Kastenmeier [3], contained a provision that permitted the taping off-air, making a captioned version within the confines of the institution and loaning to similar institutions in order to provide services for the deaf and hearing impaired.

8. Educational institutions are expected to establish appropriate control procedures to maintain the integrity of these guidelines.

The preceding Fair Use guidelines hold great moral weight in terms of providing the courts with direction, but technically they are not based in law. Strict adherence to the guidelines is critical when operating under quasi-legal conditions. It is suggested that if your institution cannot establish an adequate monitoring and enforcement system, then there might be a danger of infringement in implementing these guidelines.

At Home for Institutional Use

The privilege for institutional taping was interpreted to mean that the recording actually had to take place on the premises of the institution. Legal opinions, such as the one from the well known copyright attorney, Ivan Bender, who wrote for the TLC GUIDE, make it appear that it may be possible to tape at home and bring into school as long as all of the institutional off-air taping guidelines are followed. This means that a tape made at home would be subject to the same educational off-air taping guidelines as though it actually had been taped at the school, college, or university site. The programs may not be retained by the individual who taped them, since the individual is now operating under the guidelines for education and not the privilege for home videotaping for private performance, which was established by the U.S. Supreme Court decision in the Sony Betamax case.

Several notes of caution, however. One of the requirements for institutional taping is that if the guidelines are implemented, that such taping be monitored in order to be in compliance. If your institution intends to permit a program taped at home to be brought into the classroom, it will need to develop a tracking system which guarantees compliance with the guidelines. Secondly, there are no court cases or legal guidelines indicating that home taping for school use actually is permissible, although the opinions cited earlier are highly respected. Thirdly, although not directly related to copyright, is the situation whereby inappropriate materials are taped off-air and shown before a class. Educational institutions that allow programs taped at home to be brought into the classroom need to follow the congressional committee guidelines and adhere to the institutions' own materials selection policy.

Taping From Cable and Satellite

©IMSI

Off-air taping, under the institutional guidelines, permits the taping of "broadcast programs" which are defined as those programs transmitted by television stations without charge to the general public. Only those cable programs also available from open air broadcast in your area may be taped. (Pay services such as out-of-town stations, HBO, and Cinemax do not fall under these guidelines)

According to present interpretation, satellite transmissions would fall under the same criteria as that for cable. Currently, there are no prohibitions against receiving a signal from a satellite, except those that are scrambled, but copyright becomes an issue once taping or retransmission of the satellite programming takes place. Satellite transmission and distribution also is governed by the Communications Act (Title 47, U.S. Code) and falls under the jurisdiction of the Federal Communications Commission. Educational agencies that desire to record and/or distribute satellite signals via closed circuit systems should obtain a license to do so from the appropriate agency providing the programming.

It should be noted that a number of instructional programs, including in-service, are being provided via satellite. In many instances, fees are associated with such programs. The taping and use of these programs, without payment of the appropriate fee, would be illegal.

In addition, in 1984, the United States joined the Brussels Satellite Convention. This is a treaty in which the United States has agreed to prevent unauthorized interception and distribution of satellite signals from foreign countries. Educational institutions desiring to utilize satellite programming should negotiate rights with the appropriate copyright holders or appropriate foreign government offices regulating transmissions from their countries.

Closed Circuit Television Transmissions

Copyright holders of audiovisual works are protected from unauthorized public performance of their works. Section 110(1) of the copyright law provides a specific classroom exemption from the performance right, allowing the showing of motion pictures and other audiovisual works for the purpose of "face-to-face teaching activities."

In attempting to clarify the limitation of the terms "face-to-face" and whether this must be interpreted literally, clarification is found in the House of Representatives report in relation to this section of the law. The intent of this exemption is to allow the use of motion pictures and other audiovisual works for classroom instructional purposes, on-site. As long as the instructor and pupils are in the same building, the exemption would extend to using electronic devices for amplifying sounds and transmitting images. Section 110(1), therefore, doesn't require that the teacher and students must be able to see each other, but it does require their simultaneous presence in the same place. The exemption only extends to materials that are used instructionally, and would not apply to programs of which the content is primarily of a dramatic or entertainment nature.

By definition, this exemption would **exclude** closed circuit, ITFS or cable transmissions **between** buildings or campuses. There continues to be mixed opinions as to using copyrighted materials on a closed circuit system **within** a building. At this point, a consensus of opinion appears to permit using video programs, for instructional purposes only, within a building. (Within a building would include all buildings making up a single school, such as a high school. It would not include a campus consisting of more than one school)

Caution must be taken to determine if any of the programs, that are desired to be used, were acquired with closed circuit rights or are restricted from distribution. It cannot be assumed that all materials may be legitimately distributed through a closed circuit system. Therefore, one cannot give a blanket "yes" or "no" statement in regard to this area of media use. A number of the major audiovisual distributors sell their DVD's and videocassettes with direct performance rights only and charge an extra fee for closed circuit transmission privileges.

It is important that one carefully reads all contracts and the conditions of the purchase agreement before assuming that one may employ the Section 110(1) exemption. Quite often these performance limitations are found in very small print on the ordering information page of an audiovisual catalog. One way to provide some limited protection for yourself and your institution is to state, on your purchase order, your intent to use the material for closed-circuit distribution in your building. If the order is filled, you have a document that can be used to support a challenge of copyright infringement. However, keep in mind that such orders need to be placed with producers/distributors that have the authority to grant such rights. In general, jobbers are not usually in that position.

NOTE: Many states negotiate rights for their educational institutions in relation to specific instructional series and provide such programming via on-air transmission or videotape, with permission for use on closed circuit systems, ITFS and duplication. Check with your state department of education, higher education governing board or state library system to verify existing rights in materials being provided.

Using CopyrightedVideocassettes/DVD'sWith The "Home Use Only" Warning Label (Schools & Libraries)

©Microsoft Clip Art

Purchasing - If an educational institution **purchases** a copy of a videocassette/DVD bearing the warning label FOR HOME USE ONLY, it is permissible to use the program for face-to-face instruction with students as per Section 110(1) of the Copyright Law. The key is that the program is incorporated as part of the systematic teaching activities of the program in which it is being used. It may not be performed for other than instructional purposes unless a specific agreement is entered into at the time of purchase. The Section 110(1) performance exemption, pertaining to the videocassettes with a warning label, has been confirmed by the Motion Picture Association of America, which represents a large number of the producers who are marketing materials in the video format. These rights may be confirmed by writing to the office of the attorneys representing the Association.[4]

Libraries acquiring video collections should also be aware that public performance rights do not automatically come with the programs. Libraries are not restricted in loaning programs to patrons, unless the library has entered into a purchasing agreement that restricts such use. If a library wishes to make programs available for public viewing, individually or in a group, for other than direct instructional purposes, then public performance rights would need to be obtained. **(See Chapter 4 - Public Performance Rights)** In order to assure obtaining such rights, it is recommended to state in writing, either on a purchase order or institutional letterhead, that the stated items for purchase and the purchase price include public performance rights. If informal purchasing takes place, a letter should be obtained from the vendor indicating what specific viewing rights accompany the purchase. Any further rights, such as use on a closed circuit system or the right to duplicate will need to be stated separately.

Renting - In general, the **rental** of a videocassette bearing the FOR HOME USE ONLY warning notice and intended for instructional use would also fall under the Section 110(1) performance exemption of the Copyright Act.

However, if the school or individual signs a membership form or membership card on which a statement is made that "rentals are for home use only", this brings into play the issue of contract law. Basically, when one rents,they agree to all conditions of the rental agreement, stated or implied. The warning notice label is clearly stated. A recommendation, for limited protection, is to obtain a release statement from the rental agency granting permission for instructional use of the program. In actuality, the rental agent is not the copyright holder and does not have the authority to grant performance rights. However, by signing such a form or letter, the rental agency could become a "contributory infringer" in a copyright lawsuit for having granted such rights. Therefore, a local decision needs to be made as to whether to follow this procedure. The benefit is that it does put the rental agency on notice and often leads them to pursue whether or not their distribution license or agreement permitted public performances in an educational setting.

In any case, either purchased or rental video programs may not be used for other than planned, direct, instructional activities. They may not be used for entertainment, fund raisers or time fillers. (The Friday afternoon special!) Any use, other than instructional, would have to be negotiated at the time of purchase or rental, usually in the form of a licensing agreement. In addition, duplication or any form of copying of the videocassette or transferring from one format to another would require permission.

If the school or individual does not sign any form of rental agreement or membership form restricting the use of the "Home Use Only Videos", then these videos may be used in the classroom, for instructional use only. If the desire is to utilize a video for reward, motivation, entertainment or as a fund raiser, then public performance rights **must** be obtained to do so. There is no automatic exemption in the law for libraries or educational institutions that permit such activities.

Licensing Sources for Public Performance in Schools/Public Libraries

Licensing of "Home Use Only" video programs for use in public shools and in libraries may be obtained from:

Movie Licensing USA
201 South Jefferson Avenue
St. Louis, MO 63103-2579
888-267-2658 (Public Libraries)   877-321-1300 (Public Schools)
FAX: 877-876-9873
www.movlic.com

Motion Picture Licensing Corporation
5455 South Centinela Avenue
Los Angeles, CA 90066-6970
800-462-8855
FAX: 310-822-4440
www.mplc.com

Instructional Broadcasting

Educational institutions sometimes wish to transmit programs to classrooms via closed circuit television, between buildings via cable or ITFS (Instructional Television Fixed Service) systems, or to provide such programming directly into homes or worksites. In general, these constitute public performances and would require obtaining appropriate licenses. However, under the following specific circumstances, governmental and educational institutions have special exemptions. These exemptions were expanded by the passage of the TEACH Act, which modified the law to recognize digital as well as analog transmissions. **(Also see Chapter 11, The Internet and Distance Learning)**

Transmission/Performance

As a specific exemption to the law, transmitted performances of nondramatic literary and musical works or displays as well as **limited portions** of any other work or display of a work comparable to that typically displayed in the course of a live, classroom session, would be permitted if:[5]

1. The performance or display is a "regular part of the systematic, mediated instructional activities of a governmental body or an accredited, nonprofit educational institution.

   This section of the law is further clarified in the House Report, p. 81 & 83, where a performance is not considered an instructional activity if it is given for the recreation or entertainment of any part of the audience, rather than for their education, regardless of the educational or cultural content.

   As to the requirement that such activities be systematic, the House Report indicates that this is intended as the general equivalent of curriculums, but could be broader such as using systematic teaching methods not related to specific course work.

2. The performance or display is directly related and of material assistance to the teaching content of the transmission.

3. The transmission is made solely for and the reception limited to:

   a. students officially enrolled in the course for which the transmission is made.

   b. reception by officers or employees of governmental bodies as part of their official duties or employment.

   The House Report indicates that the intent of this section was to apply to " Government personnel who are receiving training as part of their official duties or employment." The term "government" includes federal, state and local.

4. The transmitting body or insitutution must:

   a. institute policies regarding copyright; provide information to faculty, students and relevant staff accurately describing and promoting compliance with US Copyright law.

   b. provide notice to students that materials used in connection with a course may be subject to copyright protection.

5. The transmitting body or institution must, in the case of digital transmissions:

   a. apply technological measures that reasonably prevent the retention of a work, in an accessible form, by the recipients of the transmission, for longer than the class session.

    b. act to prevent the unauthorized, further dissemination of the work, in accessible form, by recipients.

    c. not engage in conduct that could reasonably be expected to interfere with the technological *(protection)* measures, used by the copyright owners, to prevent such retention or unauthorized, further dissemination.

Transmission/Performance to Handicapped

Another exemption may be found in Section 110(8) of the Copyright Law, which permits the performance of a **nondramatic literary work**, by or in the course of a transmission specifically designed for and primarily directed to blind or other handicapped persons who are unable to read normal printed material or deaf or other handicapped persons who are unable to hear the aural signals accompanying a transmission of visual signals, if:

1. the performance is made without any purpose of direct or indirect commercial advantage.

2. the transmission is made throught the facilities of a governmental body, a noncommercial, educational broadcast station, a radio subcarrier authorization or a cable system.

Recordings Made of Instructional Transmissions

When a governmental or non-profit agency transmits a program, ahering to the requirements in the law for such transmissions, it may wish to record the program so that it may be used again for further transmissions or to be distributed to other agencies who might also carry the transmission. An example of this activity might be an educational institution that transmits the program campus-wide, but provides copies to several cable companies for transmission to home locations for students who cannot attend during the daytime. The following special recording exemption is drawn from sections 110(2) and 112(b) of the Copyright Law.

"A governmental body or other non-profit organization may make and distribute to similar organizations, for a period of seven years, without payment of royalty, thirty copies or phonorecords of a particular transmission of a program embodying the performance or display , provided that within seven years from the date of the first transmission of the program to the public, all copies are destroyed, except for one that may be preserved exclusively for archival purposes."

The preceding privilege is limited to the making of the thirty copies and no additional copies may be reproduced. The reference to "similar organizations" refers, in general, to other educational broadcasting facilities. However, an educational institution may utilize the facilities of a private cable company for distribution of qualifying programs, since the non-profit educational institution is working in conjunction with the cable company.

Recordings Made of Transmissions to Handicapped Individuals

Governmental bodies or other nonprofit organizations entitled to transmit programming to the handicapped, under Section 110(8) of the Copyright law, are permitted to make no more than ten[6] copies or phonorecords embodying the performance and to permit the use of such copies by other governmental bodies or nonprofit organizations entitled to transmit a performance of a work, under. under Section 110(8), if:

1. any such copy or phonorecord is retained and solely used by the organization that made it, or by the governmental body or nonprofit organization entitled to transmit the performance.

2. if no further copies are made.

3. the governmental body or nonprofit organization permitting any use of the copy or phonorecord made, under this subsection, does not charge for such use.

   Note: There is no direction, in this subsection of the law, requiring that any or all of these copies must be destroyed.

Fair Use Questions/Situations

Use of Donated Video Programs

A parent donates several video programs to an elementary media center collection. May these tapes be used in the school?

They may be used within the same limits as if the items had been purchased by the school. The programs may only be used in classrooms for instructional purposes tied to curriculum objectives. They may not be used for entertainment, solely for motivation or reward, or in programs i.e. latchkey, which are not tied to the regular, instructional curriculum. The tapes may be loaned to all those individuals who are eligible to borrow materials from the media center, but the borrowers should be notified that the programs do not carry public performance rights and therefore should not be shown in public places.

Conversion of Video Formats

A college has purchased a number of video programs on 3/4" tape. The playback equipment is aging and instructors have asked that the programs be converted to 1/2" VHS or digital media. Since this is a transfer from video to video, is this legal?

Copyright protects format. 3/4", 1/2" and digital, such as DVD, are separate formats of the video medium. Permission should be obtained from the copyright holder prior to converting materials from one operating format to another. This response assumes that the 3/4" programs were not purchased as "masters" with duplication rights. In that case, it would be permissible to make copies in the 1/2" medium, within the limits of the purchasing license agreement. However, the conversion to digital format would require prior permission, unless the license specifically referenced this format.

Use of Free Loan Video Rental Programs

A neighborhood video rental store is providing free loans for use in schools. Since the videos are not being rented, may they be used in the classroom or for an assembly?

It would be permissible to use them for instructional purposes, tied to curriculum and meeting instructional objectives. However, it would not be permissible to use them for entertainment, either in a classroom or in a large group setting. The neighborhood rental store is not the copyright holder and does not have the authority to grant public performance rights, which are required in order to publicly perform copyrighted material for entertainment purposes.

Use of Rental Video Programs in the Classroom

Is it legal to play a videocassette program in a classroom, labeled "For Home Use Only," that a school rented from a local, neighborhood video store?

This is a two-part answer. According to section 110(1) of the copyright law, educators are permitted to publicly perform copyrighted material for the purpose of face-to-face instruction. The key is that the tape is incorporated as part of the systematic teaching activities of the class in which it is being used. It may not be performed for other than instructional purposes, unless a specific public performance license is obtained, which generally is not available from neighborhood rental stores, since they are not the copyright holders of the material.

Secondly, the rental of a videotape might possibly constitute a contractual agreement, which would supersede copyright, thereby not permitting a performance in the classroom. Therefore, rental videocassettes with the "home use only" warning label may be used in the classroom for instructional purposes only (not entertainment, filler, motivation, reward, etc.) as long as one has not entered into a formal rental agreement restricting such use.

Teacher Rental and Use of Video Program in Classroom

May a teacher personally purchase or rent a videotape and use it in the classroom?

A teacher may use a purchased videotape in the classroom for instructional purposes only, tied to instructional objectives and curriculum. The programs may not be used for entertainment, reward, motivation or filler. If the video program was rented and a membership card or agreement was signed limiting the use of the programs to "Home Use Only", then the rental contract would take precedent over the educational exemption in the law and the video program would not be able to be used.

Videotaping Students Performing Copyrighted Works

Is it permissible to videotape students performing a copyrighted play in an auditorium so that it may be shown later to other groups in the school and used at an open house?

If the play itself is copyrighted or if there is copyrighted background music used, then it would not be permissible without obtaining prior permission from the copyright holders.

There is one exception to the preceding, however. Students may be taped in order to critique their performance. That means the recording may only be used in a showing to those students who could not see themselves perform and for the purpose of assisting them with improving their performance.

Production and Sale of Original Drama Production

Students in a drama class have written an original play and have created original music to accompany the performance. They would like to videotape the play and sell the program to other schools as a fund raiser. Since there is no copyright violation of any type taking place, would this be permissible?

This is an interesting situation. In fact, there is no violation of any copyright holders' rights, unless the students have based their work on someone else's work. Assuming all the material is original, there would be no copyright violation taking place. However, several issues may now be involved.

Does anyone intend to claim copyright to this production? The educational institution would have a potential claim if the play and/or music was produced using institutional equipment or materials and on institutional grounds. If not, the students could claim copyright if all the work was done totally away from the institution on their own time. If the students copyrighted the material, the potential exists that they could sell it for a profit, separate from their contribution to the school. If that is the case, then any copies of tapes produced with taxpayer money could not be used for that purpose since the tax supported institution would be subsidizing a private venture.

Finally, in the K-12 sector, the privacy legislation (FERPA) might come into play if students' parents did not sign a release giving permission for their children to be taped for the program or did not "opt out" of the release of Directory Information under FERPA.

How to Use A Video Program for Entertainment, Reward, Motivation

If our school desires to use a video for entertainment, reward or as a motivational technique, how can that be done since all the guidelines indicate "for instructional use only?"

In terms of reward or motivation, there is the possibility of "Fair Use" if the materials are used as part of an actual, instructional activity. As an example, if the videos are used as part of a behavior modification program and the program is clearly instructional in nature, tied in with curriculum objectives and the videos are not simply being used as a reward, it may meet the Fair Use criteria. However, keep in mind that the law clearly doesn't permit using materials for entertainment, reward or motivation due to the fact these approaches are not viewed as generally being directly instructional in nature.

Some producers of video materials, aimed at the educational market, will sell a school a "public performance right" as part of the purchase price. If this right is being offered, it will usually appear on the order information page of the vendor's catalog. In general, materials designed specifically for entertainment may be purchased or rented with public performance rights, upon request, from an agency empowered to grant such rights. However, the purchase of an entertainment video from a neighborhood video store, supermarket or discount house does not come with public performance rights and these types of stores are not licensed to grant such rights.

There are licensing agencies that represent a number of producers and provide licenses for schools and libraries. As long as you obtain a license from one of these firms, you may utilize any source, such as loan, purchase, rental, gifts, etc. to acquire your legitimate copies of video programs covered under the performance license. (See section "Licensing Sources for Public Performance Use" in this Chapter)

Guest Presenters and Video Use Rights In The Classroom

Teachers sometimes invite parents or community members to make presentations to their students. Some of these guests arrive with a videotape they wish to show as part of their activity. Is there any problem with permitting them to show the programs?

When a parent or community member is invited to make a presentation to a class, copyright law views them as "instructors" during the time they are with the group and extends the privileges granted to educators to publicly perform copyrighted materials for the purpose of "face-to-face" instruction. Therefore, they are governed by the same use restrictions that apply to the full-time teacher. They may show videos that are directed toward instruction and tie-in with instructional objectives related to class activities. The copy of the program they are using must have been legitimately obtained, and if they taped the program off-air, then it is governed by the 10 day use, 45 day erasure requirement, the same as that applies to all educational institutions. Just as teachers are restricted from showing entertainment videos, without having obtained prior permission, so are invited guests.

Loan of Video Programs Between Schools

Is it legal for one school to purchase a specific video title, then loan it to another school in the same system?

In general, the answer is yes. There may be some circumstances in which the purchase agreement, contract or purchasing terms may have included restrictions limiting its use to a specific site location. However, this type of situation is rare, although the purchasing conditions/contracts should be read carefully before acquiring any audiovisual or computer related media.

Use of Video Programs on Closed Circuit Systems

If an educational institution purchases or rents a videocassette, is it permissible to transmit the program on a closed-circuit system within a building?

This area is in a "gray zone" since the law seems to prohibit such activity, while portions of the law pertaining to exemptions for educators may be interpreted more broadly so as to permit such use. What is clear is that transmissions on closed circuit systems that go beyond the grounds of an individual school site would require permission or licensing. In general, it is recommended that the rights to perform on a closed-circuit system be obtained from the copyright holder, although it should be noted that a number of educational suppliers provide such rights. Careful reading of purchase agreements and sales literature is recommended in order to be aware of privileges and restrictions.

Taping and Redistribution of Satellite Programs

May a high school tape a program from satellite for the purpose of delayed distribution throughout the school?

The off-air taping guidelines only permit taping from open-air broadcast sources available, without charge, in the community. Satellite programming does not fit this description, with the exception of privileges granted directly by the copyright holders to educators in regard to specific programs being offered. In general, licenses are required to tape from satellite and then perform on a closed circuit system.

Demonstration of Digital Special Effects

May an instructor, in a live, direct instructional mode, utilize a digital, special effects unit to change scenes on a copyrighted video program in order to demonstrate these enhancement techniques to a class?

Yes, as long as it is a live demonstration for instructional purposes and no recording of the modifications are made. If such a recording were made, this would constitute a derivative work based upon the author's original work and would be in violation of the protection offered under the copyright law.

Modifying a Sound Track to Accompany a Play

A music sound track to a copyrighted video program is modified, electronically, to add special effects so that the sound track may be used to accompany a play performance.

This would not be permissible. This would result in creating a derivative work based upon the author's original work and would also violate the public performance rights of the author.

Use of Foreign, Copyrighted Video Programs

While traveling in England, a teacher purchased a copy of a videotape to use in a world cultures study class and for a club meeting sponsored by the teacher. The program was copyrighted in England, but showed no U.S. copyright. Could the teacher assume that she could do what she wished with the program?

In March of 1989, the United States joined the Berne Union, an international agreement, in which the member countries agree to treat the nationals of other countries like their own, for the purposes of copyright protection. Therefore, a teacher would be able to use the video for direct, classroom instruction, but would not be able to use it in a club situation, since this would be considered a public performance and would require prior permission of the copyright holders.

Students Taping From Cable For Use In Classroom

Students in a broadcast journalism class wish to use clips from movies, recorded at home, taken from cable television channels, for the purpose of critical review as part of their school/college newscast. Is this permissible?

In general, this would not be considered permissible. The off-air taping guidelines, for education only, permit taping from open air broadcast stations. Exceptions would be for programming, on cable, for which the cable company or the copyright holder has provided recording rights for educational use. In addition, most of the movies provided on cable have very specific taping restrictions. However, if very small segments are utilized, this application might fall under the general concept of Fair Use.

Use of PTA Purchased Videos For Reward/Instruction

A PTA purchased an entertainment video to show to students as a reward. The program also tied in with a unit the 5th grade was doing on oceanography. May the video be used for both of these purposes?

As a reward, the video may be loaned to students, but may not be shown in school, as this would constitute a public performance not considered instructional, and requiring prior permission. However, if the video can be directly tied into instructional objectives in the oceanography unit, then it could be used for instructional purposes.

Student Absence During 10 Day Use Period of Off-Air Programs

Following the off-air taping guidelines, if a student is absent during the 10 day use period, may we show the video to the student upon their return?

Technically, no, since the guidelines permit a video, taped off-air, to only be used with students during the 10 consecutive days following the off-air taping.

Digitizing Video Sources and Placing on a Digital, Video Server

Our district is having a digital, video server installed. The vendor has indicated there is no problem converting our currently owned, video collection to digital format and placing on the server for access throughout the district. Is this really permissible under copyright?

The technical capability to convert analog material to digital format or to make copies of digital material to place on a server doesn't necessarily mean these activities are legal.

Assuming that the original video sources are copyright protected and are legitimately owned copies, this raises several issues. One is that of converting one format to another, which potentially violates the author's right to have a derivative work created based upon their work. In fact, copyright doesn't protect ideas, but rather the format in which the ideas are expressed.

The second potential violation is that of a transmission over the network. Most educators are familiar with the need to obtain a network license for copyrighted software placed on a network or for a license to transmit video programs beyond a single site. The same concept applies to placing video materials on a digital network. Currently educators have some limited privileges to digitize and transmit in the area of distance learning, as a result of the TEACH Act. However, the act clearly does not permit the digitizing of entire, copyrighted works and use, in a transmission, is limited to the time period equivalent to a class session, not several weeks or an entire semester. If the desire is to store complete works on the server and have them available on demand, prior permission or licensing must be obtained.

Home Use vs. School Version Video Programs for Instructional Use

Our school would like to purchase a video program. The problem is that there are two versions, one labeled "for home use only" and costs about $38.00 and the other is the "school version" and costs approximately $100.00. Since this would be used for "face to face instruction," can we legally purchase the cheaper version?

The "Home Use Only" restriction does not diminish the privilege granted educators in Section 110(1) of the copyright law to publicly perform or display copyrighted material for face-to-face instruction. However, the $ 100.00 version may come with general public performance rights that would enable use for non-instructional purposes, if desired, or may permit closed circuit distribution use. Neither of these uses is permissible with the "Home Use Only" copy.

Creating a Satire of a Television Show or Commercial

If students are creating a satire of a television show or a commercial, is it necessary to obtain copyright permission?

Satire, burlesque and parody are generally regarded as Fair Use, and do not require prior permission as long as a substantial portion of the original material is not used.

However, in reference to commercials, many advertisements contain trademarked symbols or statements. It is generally viewed as fair use when primarily describing a product or simply referencing the product. A number of court cases have found parody to be permissible if the parody was neither disparaging nor obscene. Any use that would cause confusion in relation to the actual trademark or would result in a negative image to that trademark would not be viewed as fair use. Court's are more likely to find a parody to be fair use if the parody is in the form of protected free speech, rather than being commercial in nature.

Using Copyrighted Music on a Cable Access Channel

A student group has produced a PowerPoint presentation that was accompanied by background music played directly from a CD. The presentation was videotaped and now we wish to air this on our local, cable access channel to the community. Is this permissible?

There are two issues involved. First, permission would need to have been obtained to have recorded the music. Second, many local cable companies provide blanket licenses permitting the use of copyrighted music as background for productions transmitted on their access channels. You would need to verify if your cable company has an ASCAP or BMI performance license. However, if the cable company had no such license, permission would need to be obtained from the copyright holders before airing these materials on a public access channel, since this constitutes a public performance.

Using School Owned Videos in After School Programs

Can the after school program show videos that have been purchased with school funds and are included in our school video collection, i.e. videos that have been bar-coded and cataloged? The videos will be used for fillers for bad weather, etc. with no formal instruction or lesson plans.

The videos in the cataloged collection are permitted to be shown, during the regular school day, under the Section 110(1) instructional use exemption of the copyright law. This exemption doesn't apply to after school programs, unless the programs are direct extensions of the daytime curriculum and actual teaching is taking place. There is no exemption in the law for after school programs, unless they fit the definitions found in Section 110(1). Generally, most schools' after school programs do not meet the instructional criteria and such presentations constitute public performances, which require a public performance license.

Chapter 8 - Computer Software and Applications

Duplication

On December 12, 1980, by Public Law 96-517, Section 117 of the Copyright Law was amended to provide the following duplication privilege. However, since that time, this privilege has, to a great degree, become less important due to the fact that many software producers, in their documentation, permit, and sometimes encourage, the making of a "working copy" from the original.

1. A definition of a "computer program" was inserted and is defined as "a set of statements or instructions to be used directly in a computer in order to bring about a certain result."

2. The owner of a copy of a computer program is not infringing on the Copyright by making or authorizing the making of another copy or adaptation of that program if the following criteria are met:

   a. That the new copy or adaptation is created in order to use the program in conjunction with the machine and is used in no other manner.

      Permits an individual or institutional owner of a program to legally be able to modify or adapt a program to meet local needs, as long as the modification is not a major reworking of the program, and to make a copy of such program to use on their machine. Ex. Adding a printing driver to permit a program to work with a specific brand printer not included with the program.

   b. That the new copy or adaptation is for archival purposes only and that all archival copies are destroyed in the event that continued possession of the computer program should cease to be rightful.

      When an individual, library or institution purchases a software program, they are permitted to make one (1) archival or protection copy, to be held in case the working copy is destroyed or no longer functions. However, the law doesn't permit continuing to generate more replacement copies from the archival copy or to place in use, simultaneously, the archival copy and the original. (An archival copy and a backup master are not synonymous!) Any copies made, for either archival or adaptation purposes, cannot be sold, leased, given away or otherwise transferred without prior permission of the copyright owner. This is not required if the original and all copies are sold or transferred at the same time. An educational institution cannot make an adaptation of a program to meet local needs and then make multiple copies for distribution throughout the institution.

c. Any copies prepared or adapted may not be leased, sold or otherwise transferred without the authorization of the copyright owner.

Note: If the software acquired is licensed for use, rather than being owned outright, then the copy and adaptation privileges are not permitted unless the terms of the license allow such duplication.

Converting Disk Programs To CD Format

©Microsoft Clip Art

In general, changing a copyrighted work from one format to another is considered creating a derivative work, a right reserved for the copyright holder. A company producing disks and recognizing a market for CD versions could institute an infringement suit on the basis of the fourth criteria used for judging Fair Use; the effect of the use upon the potential market for or value of the copyrighted work. In addition, the making of a copy of a copyrighted computer program is restricted to that of a single archival copy, assuming the program was purchased outright.

Not withstanding the preceding statement, it may be possible to argue that the second criteria permitting the copying of a computer program, in order to modify or adapt it in order to work on the equipment that will be used, could apply to the need for making the CD copy. Also, the purchase of a disk original might be copied as a CD working copy with the disk original being retained as the one and only archival copy. However, one could not maintain both a disk and CD archival copies from an original disk copy since only one copy is permitted under the Software Act of 1980.

A safer recommendation would be to contact the copyright holder (producer) of the material desired to be converted to CD format and request permission to make this change.

Transferring Programs To Hard Disk

The same guidelines, as in the transfer from disk format to CD format would apply in the transfer to a hard disk. The hard disk versions could become the working copies with the original, purchased floppies or CD's being designated archival copies.

Please note, however, that access by users to this software may only be by means of the one computer and hard disk. Networking other computers or terminals to the one hard disk would be considered an infringement unless a networking license was obtained for each piece of copyrighted software placed on the hard disk. In addition, the preceding would only apply to software that was purchased outright. (Not licensed software, unless the agreement permitted such activity)

Networking and Multiple Machine Loading

There are no specific guidelines written into law related to networking. However, attorneys have made reference to the Computer Software Act of 1980. Congress adopted that act solely upon the recommendations based in the final report of THE NATIONAL COMMISSION ON NEW TECHNOLOGICAL USES OF COPYRIGHTED WORKS. (CONTU) In enacting CONTU's recommendations into law, they also accepted the rationale and justification for each of the positions taken. In other words, Congress enacted specific legislation, but the courts will also refer to the CONTU report for intent.

The CONTU report states "the placement of any copyrighted work into a computer is the preparation of a copy."[1] CONTU recommendations, as well as the record of Congressional committee discussions on this item, indicate that a simple transfer into memory in order to use the program doesn't constitute infringement. Once transferred through a network, however, multiple copies are created, even if they are transient in nature. The issue becomes one of whether or not these copies are "copies" in the general sense of copyright or by the definition implied in the intent of CONTU's recommendations.

Since the time of the CONTU report, it has become clear that in order to legally utilize software on a network, a network license is required. The license not only grants permission to use the software on a network, but also establishes the limits for such use.

In reference to multiple machine loading (moving from machine to machine and loading a single program into several computers for simultaneous use) The Software Copyright Act of 1980 recognized that once a program is loaded into a computer's memory, a copy is created. However, the transferring of the same program into several machines constitutes making multiple copies, which is not permitted under the law.

Use of Databases

Downloading From Remote Databases

Libraries and educational institutions, with the use of networks and telecommunications, have the ability to reach out and access electronic information from a variety of sources. These sources are often in the form of databases, which are protected by copyright law. Downloading involves the transfer of the information to some type of device in which the information can be utilized. Examples of such devices might be a microcomputer, a hard drive or a printer.

The regulations pertaining to the access and downloading of information obtained from remote databases will usually be defined in a contract with the vendor of the specific database. The contracts usually include such items as charges for "connect time," the number of citations accessed or printed, the downloading of an entire document and other conditions. If working with a vendor/jobber for multiple databases, the contract may have different stipulations dependent on the database being utilized. There are no exemptions in the law, for libraries or educational institutions, permitting downloading of database information.

Due to the fact that there are no exemptions, it would be appropriate to abide by the following guidelines:

1. Carefully review contracts or license agreements and be aware of all conditions between your library or educational institution and the vendor.

2. Do not retain extra or archival copies of a downloaded search. By doing so, one is avoiding the connect time charges and citation fees upon which the vendor derives remuneration for their efforts in providing such resources. This directly relates to the fourth criteria under Fair Use in which the user may be depriving the copyright holder of the potential market or value of their work. It would be permissible to record your search strategies for future reference.

3. The material downloaded may not be used to create a derivative work, especially if for financial gain.

4. If providing direct access to searches by students or library patrons, they should be informed of the conditions of the database contract they are searching. Posting of appropriate notices near the access station or providing a handout sheet to the user is recommended.

5. Consider the possible purchase of identical or similar database sources on CD-ROM which might prove to be less costly and would provide the ability to print citations without incurring charges.

Libraries - Creation and Distribution Of Digital Databases

Some libraries are developing digital databases, consisting of original source materials that have been digitized for access by patrons via the library's network. There are several, potential copyright infringements occurring during this process.

1. Reproduction of the author's work
2. Distribution of the author's work
3. Creation of a derivative work based on the author's work
4. Public display of the author's work

Applying the Fair Use guidelines, especially in an educational setting, one might claim the right of reproduction of a work into single or multiple copies for instructional use, drawing upon the precedent found in the photocopying guidelines. In terms of public display, the exemption for a performance of copyrighted material, for face-to-face instructional purposes, may not be met due to the fact that the instructor isn't present in the same building where the information is being presented and that the content is not necessarily directly related to the specific classroom curriculum being taught. At this point in time, lacking specific permissible guidelines, libraries attempting to develop databases from copyrighted sources, whether they be in digital, or other formats, should secure permission for the right to copy into a database and secondly, to distribute such a database through multiple copies or network access.

Libraries and Digital Reserves

Placing copies of materials on reserve in an academic library has a long history of past practice and, as indicated in the photocopying section of this guide, appears to fall under the concept of Fair Use, with certain limitations/considerations.

The act of placing an original copy of a work on reserve is not an issue. However, making a copy(ies) of works to place on reserve does, potentially, impinge on the rights granted a copyright holder. The conversion of a work into digital format continues to raise questions, both in terms of the general protection offered under copyright, as well as how the copy will be accessed. Copyright doesn't protect ideas, but rather the format in which the idea is expressed. The copyright holder is also granted distribution rights for their materials, which, in terms of the Internet, has been upheld by legislation, such as the Digital Millennium Act and TEACH Acts, each providing limited exemptions for education.

Since this continues to be an area open for legal interpretation, one should seek out legal counsel to render an opinion based upon the desired activities of your institution. You may also visit the website for the American Library Association, www.ala.org, where they have a position paper posted, in regard to digital reserves, that provides some arguments for Fair Use.

Fair Use Questions/Situations

Copying Programs for Home Use

May a building level, technology facilitator make copies of software for teachers to take home and use for class preparation? The teachers have been informed that they may make no further copies and that they are to return the copies once they have finished with their use.

In general, this would require entering into an agreement or license with the copyright holder for this purpose. The loan of the original would be legal.

Making Copies By Backing Up Hard Drives

A high school establishes a policy of daily backing up computer lab hard drives onto another hard drive, which includes programs and student data. Even though this is routinely done in many places and is suggested in the manuals accompanying hard drives, is it legal since this results in making copies of the software?

The law does not specifically address this issue, but it appears to fall in the area of Fair Use. When utilizing backup software, programs are stored in such a manner that they are not directly accessible from the backup hard drive. When the programs are stored as actual mirror copies of the original program and could be run from the backup drive, they must not be run for then two copies would be in operation. This would not be permissible unless a license agreement existed covering each and every piece of software.

Using Clip Art In A Student Newspaper That is Sold

A school has purchased several clip art disks to use with a newspaper format layout program. The students write the articles and incorporate selected clip art into the newspaper. Up to this point, the newspaper has been distributed within the school free of charge. They now would like to sell it as a fund raiser. Since they are using commercial clip art that is copyrighted, is the sale of the paper going to cause a problem?

Unless there is a specific prohibition in the purchasing literature or documentation accompanying your clip art, there would be no problem with the use indicated. In general, what is protected under copyright is the creator's right to not have someone take his/her drawings and modify, add to or reproduce in a form that would also be distributed as clip art. The intent, in providing clip art libraries, is to provide a source of drawings that may be used in a variety of applications.

Placing Already Owned Programs On A Network

A school received a small grant to purchase equipment to set up a networked, writing laboratory. The funds were not sufficient to purchase software, but the school already owns three copies of a word processing program and one copy of the page layout program to be used with students. Since these materials are already owned, may they be used on the network?

In general, software, being utilized on a network, where more than one person will access the program, requires a network license, unless such permission was provided at the time of purchase. However, copies of each of these programs could be placed on the network file server and used as a working copy, as long as only one student, at a time, can access each of the programs. The original software (discs or CD's) needs to be retained as archival copies that cannot be used on any other equipment. In the case of the word processing program, where three legitimate copies exist, if the networking software provides for restricting the number of students accessing the program and can limit the access to a maximum of three, this program could also be utilized, remembering that the three originals would have to become archival copies and could not be used on any other equipment.

In summary, without a network license, access is limited to one student for each legitimate copy of the specific software title that is owned by the school. Most schools are interested in networking to allow many students to have access to a single copy of the software title. That will require a license.

On a technical note, software may be able to be networked, (access by any user station) but may not allow several people to access the program simultaneously, if it is necessary to return to the program periodically during a session. This type of application requires multi-user software, which is what many people think they have by placing a stand-alone program on a network.

Placing Programs On More Than One File Server

A school has purchased several software packages, each with a network license. They were placed on a file server in a lab. There is a desire to equip another networked lab with an additional file server. Since a license fee has already been paid, may the programs be placed on the second file server?

In general, most license agreements restrict the use of the software to one file server and sometimes to the number of student stations served by that file server. It is important to negotiate license agreements within the context of an overall plan for the institution.

Upgrading Software and Retaining Archival Copies

A well known word processing package was purchased for use in a business education class. A legal, archival copy was made. Recently, the company has advertised an upgrade, which requires the return of all original disks. Is it permissible to keep the archival copy and use it in order to provide faculty and student access in the media center?

This is not permissible for two reasons. First, one may not retain an archival copy when they have given up ownership of the original. (This does not apply if the original or working copy was destroyed in use) Secondly, retaining the archival copy for use, in lieu of purchase of additional copies to the meet the intended needs, doesn't satisfy the "fair use" criteria and actually is one of the indicators of a copyright violation.

Backup Of Lab Pack Software & Reproduction of Documentation

An institution purchases a lab pack of a software program which included 10 copies of the disk and one copy of the documentation. Would it be permissible to make backup copies of the disks and to reproduce additional copies of the guide, but not to exceed the 10 copies of the program that had been purchased?

If the lab pack was actually purchased, not licensed or contractually restricted in any way, then it would be permissible to make an archival copy of each disk. It is not permissible to duplicate any portion of the printed documentation unless permission was granted at the time of purchase.

Screen Capture From An On-Line Database Service

A library or learning resource center subscribes to an on-line database service. The technical capability exists of "capturing the screen image from a search and saving it for later use or reprinting. Is this treated as scholarly research wherein one may copy pages from a book or reference source?

Databases are eligible for copyright protection as compilations. Since the company offering the on-line service has gathered the information and is presenting it in an organized format, any extensive copying of the database would not be considered legal. Copying to the extent permissible under the "printed materials" guidelines of the law, for the purpose of scholarly research, may fall under the category of Fair Use.

Be aware, however, that some database sources charge for downloading their information or have specific copying limitations indicated in their contracts. The contract language supersedes the copyright law.

Capturing Screen Images (Screen Dump)

An instructor desires to make a "screen dump" (a copy of what actually appears on the screen) of portions of a computer program so that it may be distributed to classes for discussion purposes in preparation for the students using the program. Is this permissible?

A "screen dump" constitutes making a copy, similar to that of photocopying material from a book or manual. Currently, there are no specific guidelines permitting such activities, as there are for printed material. However, since a computer program is defined as a literary work, the photocopying guidelines of limiting an excerpt to no more than 1000 words or 10% of the whole, whichever is less, might apply to this situation.

Reproducing Charts/Diagrams From A Computer Program

A teacher would like to reproduce selected charts and diagrams that appear in a copyrighted science program by making a copy of what appears on the screen. The copies will be distributed to students for instructional purposes.

If the individual pictures, charts, or diagrams are not copyrighted, but are simply part of a copyrighted work, then the guidelines for photocopying would apply. This permits copying, as a minimum, no more than one chart, graph, diagram or picture from a source, such as a single computer program. However, since the guidelines establish minimums, and not maximums, at issue would be how much one actually copies in relation to he whole program. Since this becomes highly interpretive, if one desires to make multiple copies from a source, permission should be sought from the copyright holder.

Loading Personally Owned Software On School Computers

An instructor purchases a copy of a simulation program for the purpose of loading onto the hard drive of a computer in his class for use with his students. Would this be permissible?

This situation would be copyright permissible if (1) the program is only loaded on this single computer (cannot be loaded on another computer at school or at home) (2) the original is kept at school as proof that the installed copy is legitimate. In addition to being copyright permissible, one would need to check if their institution permits the loading of personal software onto institutionally owned equipment.

Creating And Accessing A Library Database Program

If a library purchases a computer database program and creates a database, may it provide patron access through terminals located at branch library sites?

Even though the data itself is the property of the library, the ability to access that data from each terminal location would require the use of the program software. The search/access software would need to be licensed to operate in a network environment.

Developing Simulations/Tests Based Upon Copyrighted Content

May a mathematics teacher develop a simulated testing situation on a computer by creating a series of simulations and test questions based upon the content of copyrighted source materials (texts, workbooks) used in his/her class?

This would be considered a permissible activity since the actual copyrighted material is not being reproduced. The simulations and questions are based upon the content, not the copying of the content or questions from the copyrighted sources. Copyright protects format, not ideas.

Installation of Donated Software on School Computers

Would the Copyright law allow an elementary teacher to load, on her classroom computer, some educational software packages that the parent of one of her children donated for use with the students in her classroom? The packages are brand-new, in their original plastic wrapping.

The software could legally be installed on a school computer, in the one classroom, if the following conditions are met:

(1) That the software are all originals, not copies, and have not been installed on the donor's machine at home or other location.
(2) That there is no restriction, by a license agreement, as to location of use.
(3) That if the parent requests the return of the software, the copies installed on school

equipment must be removed.

(4) That each software title is installed on only one computer at your school, not on multiple computers.

(5) That the donated, original software be kept on site at the school as proof that the loaded, use copy was taken from an original copy.

The only other issue is a technical one. Some institutions have restricted the installation of outside software to reduce problems of conflicts with officially purchased software or for virus control. These are local issues governed by your institution's operational procedures.

©Corel Gallery

Chapter 9 - Guidelines for Educational Multimedia

GuidelinesAs Different From Law

On September 27, 1996, the Subcommittee on Courts and Intellectual Property, Committee on the Judiciary, U.S. House of Representatives, adopted a set of Fair Use guidelines for the production and use of multimedia in educational settings.[1]

As indicated in the cover letter from the Subcommittee on Courts and Intellectual Property, "These guidelines do not represent a legal document, nor are they legally binding. They do represent an agreed upon interpretation of the Fair Use provisions of the Copyright Act.... The specific portion and time limitations will help educators, scholars and students more easily identify whether using a portion of a certain copyrighted work in their multimedia program constitutes a fair use of that work. They grant a relative degree of certainty that a use within the guidelines will not be perceived as an infringement of the Copyright Act by the endorsing copyright owners, and that permission for such use will not be required. The more one exceeds these guidelines, the greater the risk that the use of a work is not fair use, and that permission must be sought."

Following is the actual text of the guidelines as adopted. Text in italics has been added for clarification.

Preparation of Multimedia Projects Using Portions of Copyrighted Works

By Students:

Students may incorporate portions of lawfully acquired copyrighted works when producing their own educational multimedia projects for a specific course.

By Educators:

Educators may incorporate portions of lawfully acquired copyrighted works when producing their own educational multimedia programs for their own teaching tools in support of curriculum-based instructional activities at educational institutions.

Permitted Uses of Educational Multimedia Programs Create Under These Guidelines

Student Use:

Students may perform and display their own educational multimedia projects, created under these guidelines, for educational use in the course for which they were created and may use them in their own portfolios as examples of their academic work for later personal uses such as job and graduate school interviews.

This section restricts the use by students, of the material they prepared, solely to the course for which it was prepared. The material may not be used for any other purpose, other than being retained for personal, portfolio use.

Educator Use for Curriculum-Based Instruction:

Educators may perform and display their own educational multimedia projects created under these guidelines for curriculum-based instruction to students in the following situations:

(1) for face to face instruction

(2) assigned to students for directed self-study

(3) for remote instruction to students enrolled in curriculum-based courses and located at remote sites, provided over the educational institution's secure electronic network in real-time, or for after class review or directed study, provided there are technological limitations on access to the network and educational multimedia project (such as a password or PIN) and provided further that the technology prevents the making of copies of copyrighted material

If the educational institution's network or technology used to access the educational multimedia project created under these guidelines cannot prevent duplication of copyrighted material, students or educators may use the multimedia educational projects over an otherwise secure network for a period of only 15 days after its initial real-time remote use in the course of instruction or 15 days after its assignment for directed self-study. After that period, students enrolled in the course may access one of the two use copies of the educational media project, placed on reserve in a learning resource center, library or similar facillity, for on-site use . Students shall be advised that they are not permitted to make their own copies of the multimedia project.

Educator Use for Peer Conferences

Educators may perform or display their own multimedia projects created under these guidelines in presentations to their peers, for example, at workshops and conferences.

The multimedia projects may be used to teach in-service classes, for presentations at faculty meetings, workshops and conferences.

Educator Use for Professional Portfolio

Educators may retain educational multimedia projects created under these guidelines in their personal portfolios for later personal uses such as tenure review or job interviews.

Limitations - Time, Portion, Copying and Distribution

Time Limitations

 © IMSI

Educators may use their educational multimedia projects, created for educational purposes under these guidelines, for teaching courses for a period of up to two years after the first instructional use with a class. Use beyond that time period, even for educational purposes, requires permission for each copyrighted portion incorporated in the production.

Students may use their educational multimedia production projects only for the duration of the course for which it was prepared.

> *If the student prepared a multimedia presentation for a one semester class, it could only be used in and for that class until the end of the semester. After that time, it could only be retained and used for personal, portfolio purposes.*

Portion Limitations

Portion limitations mean the amount of a copyrighted work that can reasonably be used in educational multimedia projects under these guidelines, regardless of the of the original medium from which the copyrighted works are taken. **In the aggregate** means the total amount of copyrighted material from a single copyrighted work that is permitted to be used in an educational multimedia project without permission under these guidelines. These limits apply cumulatively to each educator's or student's multimedia project(s) for the same academic semester, cycle or term.

> *In applying the portion limitations cumulatively, it would mean that a teacher or student is restricted to only utilizing the portions indicated below from a single, copyrighted source, as a maximum during one semester, cycle or term, no matter how many multimedia productions they produced during that period. Once one has reached the portion limitation, from a single, copyrighted work, they cannot draw upon the same copyrighted source for use in another production that occurs in the above defined period. Stated in another way, once one reaches the portion limit during the specified time period, they may no longer utilize material from that same source during that same time period.*

All students should be instructed about the reasons for copyright protection and the need to follow these guidelines. It is understood, however, that students in kindergarten through grade six may not be able to adhere rigidly to the portion limitations in this section in their independent development of educational multimedia projects. In any event, each such project retained, under the terms of these guidelines, should comply with the portion limitations in this section.

This section allows for the possibility that students in grades K-6 may not be able to rigidly adhere to the portion limits. However, once they have met the class requirements and the programs are being retained for personal, portfolio use, it is expected the productions would then be brought into compliance with the portion limitations.

Motion Media
©Corel Gallery

Up to 10% or 3 minutes, whichever is less, in the aggregate of a copyrighted motion media work may be reproduced or otherwise incorporated as part of a multimedia project created under these guidelines.

Text Material
©Microsoft Clip Art

Up to 10% or 1,000 words, whichever is less, in the aggregate of a copyrighted work consisting of text material may be reproduced or otherwise incorporated as part of a multimedia project created under these guidelines. An entire poem of less than 250 words may be used, but no more than three poems by one poet, or five poems by different poets from any anthology may be used. For poems of greater length, 250 words may be used, but no more than three excerpts by a poet, or five excerpts by different poets from a single anthology may be used.

Music, Lyrics and Music Video
©Corel Gallery

Up to 10%, but in no event more than 30 seconds, of the music and lyrics from an individual musical work (or in the aggregate of extracts from an individual work), whether the musical work is embodied in copies, or audio or audiovisual works, may be reproduced or otherwise incorporated as part of a multimedia project created under these guidelines. Any alterations to a musical work shall not change the basic melody or the fundamental character of the work.

Illustrations and Photographs
©Corel Gallery

The reproduction or incorporation of photographs and illustrations is more difficult to define with regard to Fair Use because Fair Use usually precludes the use of an entire work. Under these guidelines a photograph or illustration may be used in its entirety, but no more than 5 images by an artist or photographer may be reproduced or otherwise incorporated as part of an educational multimedia project created under these guidelines. When using photographs and illustrations from a published collective work, not more than 10% or 15 images, whichever is less, may be reproduced or otherwise incorporated as part of an educational multimedia project created under these guidelines.

Numerical Data Sets

Up to 10% or 2500 fields or cell entries, whichever is less, from a copyrighted database or data table may be reproduced or otherwise incorporated as part of a educational multimedia project created under these guidelines. A field entry is defined as a specific item of information, such as a name or Social Security number, in a record of a database file. A cell entry is defined as the intersection where a row and column meet on a spreadsheet.

Copying and Distribution Limitations

Only a limited number of copies, including the original, may be made of an educator's educational multimedia project. For all of the uses permitted, there may be no more than two "use" copies, only one of which may be placed on reserve.

An additional copy may be made for preservation purposes, but may only be used or copied to replace a use copy that has been lost, stolen, or damaged. In the case of a jointly created educational multimedia project, each principal creator may retain one copy; educators for the purposes of peer conferences and professional portfolio and students for performance and display in the course for which it was created and for personal portfolio.

A total of three copies of a multimedia production may be made. Two may actually be placed into service, only one of which may be placed on reserve. The third copy acts as a "backup master" which may be used to replace a "use" copy that has been lost, stolen or damaged.

Examples of When Permission is Required

Using Multimedia Projects for Non-Educational or Commercial Purposes

Educators and students must seek individual permissions (licenses) before using copyrighted works in educational multimedia projects for commercial reproduction and distribution.

Guidelines

Even for educational uses, educators and students must seek individual permissions for all copyrighted works incorporated in their personally created, educational multimedia projects before replicating or distributing beyond the limitations listed in the guidelines.

Distribution of Multimedia Projects Beyond Guidelines

Educators and students may not use their personally created educational multimedia projects over electronic networks, except for uses as described, without obtaining permissions for all copyrighted works incorporated in the program.

Important Reminders

Caution In Downloading Material From The Internet

© IMSI

Educators and students are advised to exercise caution in using digital material downloaded from the Internet in producing their own multimedia projects, because there is a mix of works protected by copyright and works in the public domain on the network. Access to works on the Internet does not automatically mean that these can be reproduced and reused without permission or royalty payment and furthermore, some copyrighted works may have been posted to the Internet without authorization of the copyright holder.

Attribution and Acknowledgment

Educators and students are reminded to credit the sources and display the copyright notice © and copyright ownership information, if this is shown in the original source, for all works incorporated as part of the educational multimedia projects prepared by educators and students, including those prepared under Fair Use. Crediting the source must adequately identify the source of the work, giving full bibliographic description where available (including author, title, publisher, and place and date of publication). The copyright ownership information includes the copyright notice (©, year of first publication and name of the copyright holder).

The credit and copyright notice information may be combined and shown in a separate section of the educational multimedia project (e.g. credit section) except for images incorporated into the project. In such cases, the copyright notice and the name of the creator of the image must be incorporated into the image when, and to the extent, such information is reasonably available; credit and copyright notice information is considered "incorporated" if it is attached to the image file and appears on the screen when the image is viewed. In those cases when displaying source credits and copyright ownership information on the screen with the image would be mutually exclusive with an instructional objective (e.g. during examinations in which the source credits and /or copyright information would be relevant to the examination questions), those images may be displayed without such information being simultaneously displayed on the screen. In such cases, this information should be linked to the image in a manner compatible with such instructional objectives.

Notice of Use Restrictions

Educators and students are advised that they must include, on the opening screen of their multimedia program and any accompanying print material, a notice that certain materials are included under the Fair Use exemption of the U.S. Copyright Law and have been prepared according to the multimedia Fair Use guidelines and are restricted from further use.

Future Uses Beyond Fair Use

Duplication of Multimedia Projects Beyond Limitations Listed

Educators and students are advised to note that if there is a possibility that their own educational multimedia project incorporating copyrighted works under fair use could later result in broader dissemination, whether or not as commercial products, it is strongly recommended that they take steps to obtain permission during the development process for all copyrighted portions rather than waiting until after completion of the project.

Integrity of Copyrighted Works: Alterations

Educators and students may make alterations in the portions of the copyrighted works they incorporate as part of an educational multimedia project only if the alterations support specific instructional objectives. Educators and students are advised to note that alterations have been made.

Reproduction or Decompilation of Copyrighted Computer Programs

Educators and students should be aware that reproduction or decompilation of copyrighted computer programs and portions thereof, for example the transfer of underlying code or control mechanisms, even for educational uses, are outside the scope of these guidelines.

Licenses and Contracts

Educators and students should determine whether specific copyrighted works, or other data or information, are subject to a license or contract. Fair Use and these guidelines shall not preempt or supersede licenses and contractual obligations.

Fair Use Questions/Situations

Modifying Scanned Or Digitized Images

To what degree would a scanned-in or digitized image have to be changed so that it would no longer resemble the original and, therefore, not be considered a copyright infringement?

Scanning or digitizing a copyrighted work and modifying that work, even if not recognizable when done, would be considered violating the rights of the original author/copyright holder, since their work formed the basis or starting point of the new work created. However, copyright only protects the format in which an idea is expressed, but doesn't protect the idea. If one gets an idea, by observing a copyrighted work, and then creates a work based on that idea that is not recognizable as the original work, this would not generally be viewed as an infringement.

Use of Clip Art In Multimedia, Video and Computer Programs

May clip art be incorporated into multimedia, video or computer programs created by either faculty or students?

Yes, unless there are specific restrictions accompanying the clip art material.

Importing Video Footage for a Quicktime Segment

I would like to import a portion of a videotape into a Quicktime segment to be part of a presentation I am preparing to show to my students. How much may I actually take from the original video?

Up to 10% or 3 minutes, whichever is less, *in the aggregate, of a copyrighted motion media work, may be reproduced or otherwise incorporated as part of a multimedia project created under these guidelines.

Using Text From Copyrighted Works

What are the limitations on reproducing and incorporating portions of text, for example from a short story, a poem or other text based materials?

Up to 10% or 1,000 words, whichever is less, *in the aggregate, of a copyrighted work consisting of text material may be reproduced or otherwise incorporated as part of a multimedia project. If the original work is a poem of less than 250 words, the entire poem may be used, but no more than three poems by one poet, or five poems by different poets from any single anthology. Poems that are greater than 250 words are limited to a maximum of 250 words used with no more than three excerpts from a single poet, or five excerpts by different poets from a single anthology. (Note: these are the same conditions found in the Fair Use guidelines for the photocopying of materials)

Using Copyrighted Music In A Multimedia Production

Is it permissible to incorporate copyrighted music, lyrics or music taken from a music video into a multimedia production?

Up to 10%, but in no event more than 30 seconds, of the music and lyrics from an individual musical work (or *in the aggregate of extracts from an individual work) may be reproduced or incorporated as part of a multimedia project. The music may be taken from the copy of an actual musical work or from an audio or audiovisual work such as a CD, music video, etc. Any alterations to a musical work shall not change the basic melody or the fundamental character of the work.

Using Photographs and Illustrations In A Powerpoint Presentation

I would like to include in my PowerPoint presentation several photographs and illustrations taken from books, magazines and other copyrighted sources. Do the guidelines provide for this type of activity?

Under these guidelines a photograph or illustration may be used in its entirety, but no more than five images by a single artist or photographer may be reproduced or otherwise incorporated into an educational multimedia project. When using photographs and illustrations from a published collective work, not more than 10% or 15 images, whichever is less, may be reproduced or otherwise incorporated into the production.

Using Information From Databases and Spreadsheets

As part of the preceding PowerPoint presentation, I would also like to include some data fields taken from several copyrighted spreadsheets and databases. What are the limits on the number of these fields that I may utilize?

You may reproduce or incorporate into your production up to 10% or 2500 field entries, whichever is less, from a copyrighted database or data table. A field entry is defined as a specified item of information, such as a name or Social Security number, in a record of a database file. A cell entry is defined as the intersection where a row and a column meet on a spreadsheet.

Permissible Copies of Finished, Multimedia Productions

When I, or one of my students, complete a multimedia project, how many copies can be made?

Two "use" copies may be made, only one of which is permitted to be placed on reserve. A third copy may be made for preservation purposes (backup copy), but may only be used or copied to replace one of the two use copies that has been lost, stolen or damaged. If more than one person produced the multimedia program, each principal creator is permitted to retain one copy for the purposes defined in the Guidelines.

[*   In the aggregate means the total amount of copyrighted material from a single copyrighted work that is permitted under these guidelines. The limits apply cumulatively to each educator's or student's multimedia project(s) for the same academic semester or term.]

© Microsoft Clip Art

Chapter 10 - DVD/CD-ROM & Laserdisc

At the beginning of this guide, a definition was provided as to the scope of copyrighted works, which included "any tangible medium of expression, now known or later developed, which can be perceived, reproduced, or otherwise communicated, either directly or with the aid of a machine or device." The copyright law does not attempt to address each form of hardware/software with specific guidelines for appropriate use. Instead, the law, combined with court cases, provides a structure in which to address the more recent information technologies, some of which have been dealt with in separate sections found in this manual. With the lack of specific guidelines, one must refer to the rights of the author combined with the Fair Use guidelines. **(Also see Chapter 9, Fair Use Guidelines for Educational Multimedia)**

CD-ROM Technology

© IMSI

The advent of the Compact Disk-Read Only Memory (CD-ROM) storage of large amounts of printed and graphic material has led to the release of bibliographic and research based source materials such as the Wilson Indexes, Groliers Encyclopedia, Comptons Encyclopedia, ERIC documents and others. When an institution purchases such an item, the database may be accessed as a reference source. As such, faculty and students may copy sections as per the guidelines for the reproduction of the other printed materials for the purpose of research and teaching. **(See Chapter 3, Photocopying)** Keep in mind that all copies or printouts become the property of the patron or student, not the library.

To provide greater patron access, it may be desirable to network multiple computers to address one CD-ROM reader/player and its software. Currently, the consensus of legal interpretations is that unless the database information is in the public domain, this would be considered an infringement in lieu of the purchase of multiple copies for more than one reference station. What would be required would be the purchase of a network license for each CD-ROM product placed on the network.

In addition to the network license, there are some vendors who are licensing, rather than selling, stand-alone application packages. Since contract law supersedes copyright, the following need to be taken into consideration when purchasing CD-ROM products:

1. Carefully read all contracts prior to purchase. Make sure the conditions under which you wish to operate the CD-ROM program are covered. Do not hesitate to negotiate the rights that are desired. It is much more difficult to do so after purchase. As examples, you may desire to network or to maintain use of older editions when new editions are released.

2. If you currently own CD-ROM products, carefully review any contracts for specific

conditions or limitations on use and also note such conditions if they exist in the vendor's purchasing catalog or advertising sheet.

DVD and LaserdiscTechnology

© Microsoft Clip Art

Digital video disks (DVD's) and laserdiscs have many of the characteristics of videocassettes, and all are considered audiovisual mediums protected under copyright. It should be kept in perspective that although as technologies become more sophisticated and provide the user with greater ease in which to copy and merge with other technologies, that the technical capability to capture audio and video images does not diminish an author's rights in their creative material. As with other mediums qualifying for copyright protection, one may only copy, prepare a derivative work, sell or lease, publicly perform or display under specific exemptions in the law or under Fair Use circumstances. Otherwise, rights must be obtained from the copyright holder.

Similar to the general video medium, if a small portion was copied from a DVD or laserdisc, and was used as part of a larger work in which the copied portion constituted a very small part and the copied portion was not of a highly original nature, the application might fall under Fair Use. Copying a single image from a DVD or laserdisc to be incorporated into a videocassette segment produced by a student to meet a classroom requirement might well be considered a Fair Use application. Extensive copying of such images would not.

Fair Use Questions/Situations

Printing Articles From CD-ROM Encyclopedias & Periodicals

When students or teachers use an encyclopedia on CD-ROM, may they print out pages or articles for class assignments or for research purposes?

Most definitely! Even though the encyclopedia is now in an electronic format, it is still considered to fall under the guidelines that permit the copying of printed material for study, scholarly research and teaching. However, in both the printed and electronic versions, one may not copy the entire encyclopedia or large segments of the material.

A high school media center purchases a periodical subscription provided on a CD-ROM. May teachers and students print out articles, quotes, etc., as part of their research?

Yes. Even though appearing in another medium, the copying from periodical sources would be governed by the photocopying guidelines.

Placing CD-ROM Resources On A Network

The school owns a CD-ROM copy of a periodical. Due to its cost, it is desirable to network this program, utilizing a CD-ROM tower, to several computer stations in a media center, and to labs within the school. Is this legal?

Viewed in the same manner as networking computer software one may not do so legally without requesting permission, usually in the form of a network license. This has brought up a fundamental problem that relates to many of the newer technologies. It is often believed that because it is technically feasible to do something and the school has already invested a significant amount of money in purchasing the original software, that it ought to be permissible to use the product, in any manner, for sound, educational purposes. Sadly enough, educational rationale and the law do not mix.

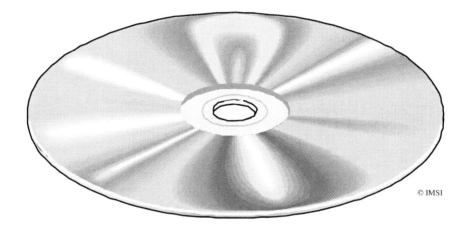

© IMSI

Chapter 11 - The Internet and Distance Learning

Guidelines for Use of the Internet

© Microsoft Clip Art

In recent years, Congress has attempted to deal with copyright, trademark and morals issues related to the use of the Internet. In this process, the rights of copyright holders have been recognized as not being diminished simply because the material may appear on the worldwide web. This was further reinforced when the United States became a signatory to the World Intellectual Property Organization Treaty, which was officially ratified by the Senate and implemented as the Digital Millennium Act. In this treaty, the member countries agreed to formally extend the rights of copyright holders to information, images, music and software distributed on the Internet. **(Also see Chapter 13, International Copyright)**

Recognizing that the rights of copyright holders pertain to materials placed on the Internet, the following guidelines are suggested in order not to become a statistic on the information superhighway!

- Assume materials are copyrighted, unless otherwise stated.
- Follow fair use precedents and guidelines set in current law. (photocopying; multimedia productions, general fair use, etc.)
- Properly cite net resources. (**see www.classroom.com/community/connection/howto/ citeresources.jhtm for bibliographic format for on-line resources**)
- Request permission when in doubt or if use will extend beyond the classroom.
- Notify webmaster or owner of a website if you intend to capture a web site with statement of reason for the need to capture. Request permission if use is beyond research or classroom presentation.

Christopher Wolf, attorney, writing for *The National Law Journal*, states "pending new technological or legislative fixes, users of the Internet need to be aware of their potential liability for copyright infringement. While the copyright laws include the flexible "Fair Use" doctrine as a protection for legitimate and reasonable use of copyrighted works, serious infringements likely will not be excused because of the newness of the medium, or because the act of infringement is simple to perform. Just because the Internet makes copying easy, doesn't mean it makes copying legal." [1]

Linking to Sites

In general, linking to another website is not viewed as a copyright infringement. However, it does offer the potential of becoming a copyright issue. One area of potential concern is that of where a link takes a viewer. If the link takes the viewer to the body of an author's work and the initial website does not inform the viewer they are being taken to another site, this may falsely give the impression that one is still on a page within the original website being viewed, thereby not giving credit to the linked site.

This acknowledgement may be accomplished in several ways.

1. In the body of text in the original viewing site, inform the viewer they are being taken to another site and specifically reference that site.
2. Link to the homepage of the linked site and provide directions to the reader of how they can navigate to the content desired.

Another possible issue, related to the very act of linking into the body of another site, is bypassing the homepage of that site. It may be possible that the author had notified readers of limitations on the use of the site, such as no downloading, printing or further distribution of the material and by linking to the body of the other author's site, the viewer is not made aware of the warnings.

For the utmost in copyright safety in linking, consider following these suggested strategies.

1. Request prior permission to link to another site. Obtain such permission in writing.
2. Instead of directly linking, create an electronic bibliography which clearly identifies the sites and their URL's. One may directly link from this bibliography or portal page.

Website Creation and Ownership

Schools and libraries, in the process of creating websites, sometimes may enlist the assistance of students or volunteers. If, in fact, these individuals are not being paid for such work and the institution has not obtained a release or entered into an agreement with these individuals by which they turn over the rights to what they have created to the institution, then that portion of the site and the content they have created to be placed on the site are the property of the student or volunteer.

In general, by way of legal precedent, employees who create copyrighted works on employer time and utilize the equipment and materials provided by he employer, do not have right of claim to ownership of that material. Therefore, if a teacher, instructor or librarian creates a website for their employer or contributes to the creation of that website, they do not have an automatic claim to the portion they have created. If an employee creates a website or content for a website on their own time with their own materials and equipment, in general, they have the right of claim to copyright for what they have created. However, some institutions are requiring that the creator turn over rights before such material is posted to a website or an employment contract may require that anything created while in the employ of that institution, no matter on work time or not, is the property of the institution. This is more typical of businesses, however, than it is of educational institutions or libraries.

Copyright and Distance Learning

Distance learning often involves the desire to transmit copyrighted works from one site to another. This may involve transmissions that take place within one school or institution or may result in establishing connections between a number of different, physical site locations. The five protections offered a copyright holder affect the use of materials for distance learning purposes. Although the concept of Fair Use may still apply, in general, the transmission of copyrighted works require permission from the copyright holders, with the following, recent and significant exception related to **instructional** transmissions in support of distance learning.

The TEACH Act

The entire section 110(2) of the Copyright Law, dealing with limited exemptions for educational transmissions, has been revised. Originally based upon the world of analog television, this section now recognizes digital transmissions and their importance in distance learning and permits such transmissions to take place, for direct, instructional purposes.

The new privileges now granted are for the delivery of "mediated instruction", a concept which views distance learning transmissions as somewhat parallel to structured classroom activities, taught within a very brief, finite amount of time. This brief time of use would be comparable to teaching a specific class session, not the period of an entire course. As such, the materials created may not be retained indefinitely for use and re-use, not even for the length of a semester class/course.

A major change is that in addition to the previous Section 110(2) exemptions permitting the performance of non-dramatic literary and musical works, the exemptions have been expanded, now permitting the performance of any other copyrighted work, including dramatic works and audiovisual works, but only in "reasonable and limited portions." Therefore, one could not perform and entire video, but only could play a segment. (Length of segment not defined) These brief segments are defined as what would be typically used in a classroom. There is some contradiction, on this point, since teachers/instructors sometimes use an entire video during a class period. However, it is very clear in the legislation that it is not the intent of the exemption to permit such full use activity to take place.

In addition to the expanded performance exemption, displays are permitted of copyrighted works "in an amount comparable to that which is typically displayed in the course of a live classroom session." This would include displaying pictures, photographs, charts, diagrams, sculpture, art, etc.

In order to transmit the distance learning sessions, utilizing copyrighted material, temporary transmission copies, in either analog or digital form may be made, including the conversion of the portions of copyrighted material from analog to digital that is permitted, under this legislation, to be included in the transmission. This conversion is only permitted if a digital version is not available to the institution or, if a digital version is available, it is secured by technology protection measures that prevent its use in a distance learning transmission.

However, it is **not** permissible to convert complete works from analog to digital or to convert from one format to another for the convenience of online access when the use of the material is not used directly as part of the distance learning class session. Therefore, it would not be permissible to convert videotapes or other analog sources to digital format for the purpose of video streaming or to set up video servers for storing copyrighted works for the purpose of access on demand, especially when such activity extends over a period of time greater than what would normally be a class session.
It is a requirement that such transmissions must be restricted to students/employees enrolled in the

course and that measures must be instituted that prevent the end user from copying or retransmitting the content of the distance learning transmission. (**Note:** This has raised a question as to the application of general Fair Use, where students are permitted to copy brief segments of material for research. This has not yet been clarified)

All performances and displays must be made at the direction of or under the actual supervision of an instructor.

Materials transmitted must be "an integral part of a class session offered as a regular part of the systematic, mediated instructional activities" of the educational institution.

As with the wording of section 110(2), prior to this revision, the copyrighted materials used must be "directly related and of material assistance to the teaching content of the transmission."

The following items are excluded from use under The TEACH ACT.

a. Works that are marketed "primarily for performance or display as part of mediated instructional activities transmitted via digital networks." Companies are now beginning to market distance learning courses, curriculums and resources and these materials, designed and marketed for education, are not permitted to be used in a distance learning situation,unless one establishes an agreement or contract with the provider.

b. Any performance or display by means of a copy(ies) "not lawfully made or acquired." and if the educational institution "knew or had reason to believe" that they were not lawfully made or acquired.

Over time, more details and clarifying interpretations will become available. At this point, educators who had desired to develop on-line courses that could be accessed anytime, any place and stored and served by video or data servers over semester/term periods of time, with the ability to repeat another semester/term or year, will find that the TEACH Act does not provide those permissions. Prior permission from copyright holders will need to be obtained. (**Also see Chapter 7, Video, under "Instructional Broadcasting"**)

Fair Use Questions/Situations

Reproducing A Newspaper Article Downloaded From A Web Site

A teacher wishes to download an article from a newspaper Web site and make copies for classroom discussion with her students. Is this permissible?

Yes, this would be permissible following the current photocopying guidelines which established precedent for making multiple copies for classroom use. (See Chapter 3, Photocopying)

Forwarding Personal E-mail Messages

You receive a personal, e-mail message from another individual. You would like to share the contents of this message and forward to several other people. Is this permissible?

One must assume that the message was sent to you as an individual and unless specifically stated, has no forwarding or copying rights. At issue, in this instance, are not only copyright laws, but also other statutes generally referred to as Privacy Acts. If you desire to share such information, you should contact the sender and request permission.

However, if the e-mail message you received was in response to a question you had posed and in that question, you had indicated that responses would be shared with others, then it would be permissible to forward the response to those so indicated when the question was sent out. Keep in mind, however, that without having clearly stated the nature of the individuals or group to whom you intended to forward the material, you may be open to litigation if, by the nature of where you forwarded the material, the reputation of the sender was impugned.

Posting and E-Mailing Magazine Articles

I have seen a wonderful article on changing technology in a magazine that I would like to e-mail to other technology coordinators in my district and around the state, as well as place on our district Web site for internal reference. If I give appropriate credit as to the source, may I share this information?

In general, this would not meet the Fair Use test and would be in violation of the rights of the copyright holder. First there is the potential violation of having made a copy by entering the text on your Web site and e-mail. Secondly, would be the potential violation of having published and making available an article from a copyrighted work without permission. It also potentially violates the fourth Fair Use criteria, which is the protection of future income, since, if this practice was to continue, it might lead to diminishing purchases of the magazine from which the articles are being copied.

Two approaches may be used to meet your desire for sharing information. One would be to write to the copyright holder requesting permission to post this article. Second, would be to simply notify your colleagues as to the title and source, providing a brief summary as to contents, so that they might pursue going directly to that source.

Use of Copyrighted Materials For Distance Learning

If a school district wishes to offer a class by closed circuit television to several schools in the district that do not have sufficient enrollment to warrant a class, may videos, computer soft ware and other media normally used by the instructor now be transmitted to all the other sites?

Within the specific limitations of the TEACH Act, portions of copyrighted works may be used in instructional transmissions. However, if the use desired doesn't meet the criteria of the law, it would not automatically be permissible to offer this or other forms of distance learning without first obtaining permission from the copyright holders, which usually takes the form of a license agreement.

Displaying Photographs, Charts, Tables

Under the TEACH Act, may a professor incorporate individual photographs, charts or tables in a distance learning class utilizing a presentation station or similar device?

Yes, this would be permissible, within the constraints of limiting the amount taken from any one source to incorporate in the transmission.

Copying from the Internet to Make Class Copies

I have a teacher who wants to use a picture of a book jacket taken from an Internet site. She wants to make multiple copies of the picture to hand out to students and to place one on a display board to use with in an instructional unit. Is this permissible?

Copying text, pictures, graphs, charts, diagrams, etc. from the Internet to make multiple copies for classroom distribution falls under the precedent set by the Photocopying Guidelines. As such, the teacher could take one or two pictures from the book, on-line, and then make copies for the class. However, if the teacher decided to keep the copies for another year or to use the same activity and source another year, permission would need to be obtained.

Copying Graphics for Use on a Website

Students have found graphics, on other websites, that they would like to include on our school's site. If the original source is given credit, is it OK to use these graphics?

A website, in and of itself, is copyright protected. This includes the graphics and content. Utilizing the graphics in a classroom environment, limited to one or two from a site, would generally meet fair use guidelines for classroom use. However, placement on the web is a form of large scale publication. It would be appropriate to seek permission prior to use.

Chapter 12 - Obtaining Copyright Permission

Since the copyright owner has the right to duplicate, create a derivative work, distribute, perform and publicly display his/her copyrighted work, and even though there are a number of prohibitions against specific uses of materials by others, the copyright owner has the right to grant permission for uses not automatically allowed under the Copyright Act. This permission is obtained under one or more of the following procedures/processes.

Writing for Permission

An individual or an institution may write directly to the copyright holder and request permission to do whatever is desired in relation to the copyrighted material. It is best to be very specific in terms of identifying the source of the material to be copied or performed, why one desires to have this privilege and clearly stating the purpose of the use and, if a reproduction, the quantities anticipated.

If the request is to change an item from one format to another, such as burning a CD from a tape, that too should be indicated. Any of the absolute prohibitions in the Copyright Law, such as not being able to duplicate pages from a consumable workbook, test booklet, scoring sheet, etc., may be overridden by the author/copyright holder, since they hold the copyright. In other words, don't be afraid to ask! At worst, one may receive a negative response. However, usual responses range from a "yes" to "yes" with special conditions or the requirement to pay a fee or royalty for the privilege.

To assist in providing the copyright holder with the appropriate information necessary to make a judgment, a **Sample Form for Writing for Copyright Permission** may be found in **Appendix C** of this guide. It may be modified in any way to make it usable for an individual or institution. The permission or denial, when returned by the copyright holder, should be maintained on file as evidence of the rights granted or rejected.

Copyright Searches

©Corel Gallery

As had been indicated in the section entitled "Out-of Print", found in Chapter 3 of this guide, the fact that an item is no longer in print or available does not negate the copyright protection for the copyright holder that exists with the material. An institution, library or an individual may not automatically proceed to making copies of out of print materials nor utilizing the material in any manner not consistent with the assumption that the item is still under copyright protection.

Sometimes it is difficult to determine who is the current copyright holder from whom to seek permission, especially if the material is no longer available. The following sources provide copyright searches, with payment of a fee required.

Reference and Bibliography Section
LM-451
Copyright Office, Library of Congress
101 Independence Avenue, SE
Washington, D.C. 20559-6000
(202) 707-6850

Government Liaison Services, Inc.
200 N. Glebe Rd., Suite 321
Arlington, VA 22203
Phone: (800) 642-6564; (703) 524-8200
FAX: (703) 525-8451
www.trademarkinfo.com

Thomson & Thomson Copyright Research Group
1750 K Street, NW, Suite 200
Washington, DC 20006-2305
Phone: (800) 356-8630; (202) 835-0240
FAX: (202) 728-0744
www.thomson-thomson.com

Licensing

Licensing is a formal contract whereby both the purchaser and the owner agree to certain conditions. If the purchaser does not comply with the license, they are open to both a lawsuit, based upon breaking a contractual agreement, and infringing upon the rights of the copyright holder. However, the license also protects the purchaser for it clearly defines the scope of the activities that are allowed.

Currently, license procedures are available for duplicating, networking and multiple machine loading of computer software, networking of CD-ROM software and the duplication and closed/open air transmission of video programs. Licensure is beginning to become available for digitizing materials in analog formats, such as tape to DVD. One should note that some companies actually do not sell their software, but only license it for use. One must take care to read sales literature carefully to determine if they are actually purchasing the software and becoming the legitimate owner with the privileges granted in the Software Act of 1980, or if they have become a licensee without these privileges. Some licenses are a one time payment and others must be renewed on a scheduled basis. The latter is typical of video series.

Licenses are required to publicly perform or display dramatic and non-dramatic literary works and musical works, with the specific exceptions outlined earlier in this guide in **Chapter 4 - Public Performance.** In contrast to other media, music and the performing arts are highly organized in regard to licensing activities and the writers, composers, authors, publishers and producers pay fees to licensing agencies that act as the clearing house for granting performance rights. It is these agencies that must be contacted to obtain a license, not the author/publisher. Those agencies that are well known in the music performance licensing area are Broadcast Music, Inc. (BMI) and the American Society of Authors, Composers and Publishers (ASCAP). Their addresses, as well as those of other agencies, may be found in the **Bibliography** in a section entitled **"Licensing Agencies/Societies."**

In general, the conditions of a license agreement are set by the agency granting the license. Some are willing to make modifications based upon the user institution's/individual's request. Prior to signing any license, this author recommends that you submit the license to your attorney of record for review and for recommendations for change to the licensing agency. State laws sometime conflict with license terms and, therefore, the license conditions will need to be amended before making a legal commitment.

PurchaseAgreements

If prior to purchasing an item, an institution desires to have certain privileges or rights, such as closed circuit transmission of videotapes or DVD's, to video stream content or the right to duplicate computer software for a laboratory setting, it would be appropriate to negotiate such rights into the purchase agreement or contract. This differs from a license in that the purchasing agency has established a condition of purchase. As an example, an institution, making a decision on a textbook adoption, might negotiate the rights to unlimited duplication of workbooks and support materials that accompany the text. Such a large scale expense, over a long period of time, places the purchasing institution in a very good position to obtain the desired privileges. This position is weakened after the purchase has taken place.

The key factor, in all of the preceding, is to negotiate the rights you desire prior to purchase!

© IMSI

Chapter 13 - International Copyright

The United States has been a participant 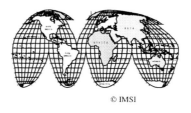 in several international agreements, all of which had their intention of protecting the works of U.S. authors in other countries while protecting the works of member foreign nationals in the United States. In July of 1914, the United States entered the Pan American Copyright Convention (treaty) and since September 1955, has adhered to the Universal Copyright Convention. The conditions of copyright protection offered the member nations were very similar to that of United States copyright law.

U.S. Joins Berne Union

On March 1, 1989, the United States entered into an international treaty, the Berne Convention, whose purpose is to protect the rights of the authors from the 79 member countries. Foreign works are protected in the United States, and the works of U.S. nationals are protected in the member foreign countries. This required some modification in United States law in order to satisfy obligations under the treaty and those changes also took effect on March 1, 1989. U.S. law continues to govern the protection and registration of works in the United States.

Effect of U.S. Membership In The Berne Union

Since members of the Berne Union agree to a certain minimum level of copyright protection, each Berne Union country provides at least that guaranteed level for U.S. authors.

Members of the Berne Union agree to treat nationals of other member countries like their own nationals for purposes of copyright. Therefore, U.S. authors will often receive higher levels of protection than the guaranteed minimum, since foreign copyright regulations are often more stringent than those in the United States.

Overall, piracy of U.S. works abroad can be fought more effectively.

Beginning March 1, 1989, works of foreign authors who are nationals of a Berne Union country and whose works were first published in a Berne Union country are automatically protected in the United States.

Subject Matter Protected By the Berne Convention

In general, the subject matter of protection under the Berne Convention encompasses any original work of authorship "in the literary, scientific and artistic domain, whatever may be the mode or form of its expression." Such works include "painting," "architecture," "photographic works to which are assimilated works expressed by a process analogous to photography," "illustrations," and "three-dimensional works relative to geography, topography, architecture or science, as well as books, dramatic or dramatico-musical works, musical compositions, and cinematographic works."

The Berne Convention requires member countries to provide protection for derivative works and collections of literary and artistic works, but protection of governmental or other official works is made optional for each member state. It excludes "news of the day" or "miscellaneous facts, having the character of mere items of press information," from the material to be protected by the Berne Convention and distinguishes between non-protectable facts and protectable original expressions containing "sufficient intellectual effort for them to be considered as literary and artistic works."

U.S. Law Amended

In order to fulfill its Berne Convention obligations, the United States made certain changes in its copyright law by passing the Berne Convention Implementation Act of 1988. These changes were not retroactive and became effective only on and after March 1, 1989.

Mandatory Notice of Copyright Is Abolished

For works first published on or after March 1, 1989, a mandatory notice of copyright is no longer required. Failure to place such notice of copyright no longer results in the loss of copyright protection.

However, it is still strongly recommended to place a notice of copyright on all published works. One of the benefits is that an infringer will not be able to claim that he/she "innocently infringed" a work. A sample notice of copyright is:

> © 2003 William Pearson

Also eliminated has been the requirement that if a portion of a copyrighted work consists of U.S. government materials that those materials had to be identified. However, if the voluntary use of the copyright notice is used, then a statement still is required as to what is actually copyrighted in the work. An example of such a notice is:

> © 2003 William Pearson. Copyright claimed in Chapters 1-12, exclusive of U.S. government documents found in Appendices A and B.

Mandatory Deposit

If continuing to voluntarily register for copyright, owners must deposit in the Copyright Office two complete copies or phonorecords of the best edition of all works subject to copyright that are publicly distributed in the United States, whether or not the work contains a notice of copyright. This requirement can be met by formally registering the material with the Copyright Office.

Registration As A Prerequisite To A Law Suit*

Before a copyright infringement suit is brought for a work of U.S. origin, it must be submitted to the Copyright Office for registration. Although Berne Convention works whose origin is not the United States are exempt from this registration requirement, the person seeking to sue bears the burden of proving that they were exempt from the registration requirement in order to be able to institute a lawsuit under the Berne Convention.

* Note: Mandatory registration for works of U.S. origin is no longer required. This change was a result of the Copyright Reform Act of 1993. (See Chapter 14, Highlights of Law Changes)

General Agreement on Tariffs and Trade (GATT)

This agreement was formally ratified in the United States on December 8, 1994, in the form of the Uruguay Round Agreements Act. The GATT agreement deals with a number of issues related to international trade, one of which is the protection of intellectual property rights, as per a subsection of the Uruguay Agreement, referred to as TRIPS (Trade Related Aspects of Intellectual Property Rights). The enactment of the agreement brought with it the following changes to U.S. Copyright Law.

Modification - Computer Software Rental Amendments Act[28]

In 1990, Congress enacted the Software Rental Amendments Act whose purpose was to further protect the copyright holders of computer software by restricting the loan or rental of computer software.[1] This exception to the first sale doctrine was scheduled to expire on October 1, 1997. In compliance with GATT, the expiration date has been repealed and the copyright holders are now protected in both the rental and sale of computer programs. In addition to the preceding, GATT has added the same protection to the distribution of movies.[2] Libraries and educational institutions continue to be exempt from these provisions as they relate to the loan of software or movies.

Protection for Live Performances

The act also makes the creation of and trafficking in bootleg recordings and videotapes of live musical performances a copyright infringement.

Re-Establishes Protection for Foreign Works

Foreign works, which previously had been looked upon as being in the public domain in the United States because they did not comply with the prior requirement of U.S. Copyright law, especially the mandatory copyright notice (which by the Berne Convention is no longer mandatory) now have their copyright protection restored, as long as those works are protected in their own "source country."

U.S. law also provided that statutory damages and attorneys fees were not available for works not registered with the U.S. Copyright Office. The Act provides such legal remedies, in addition to others, to works now restored to copyright protection, but that such remedies are effective from the date on which they were restored, not the date of registration.

Computer Programs and Compilations of Data

TRIPS explicitly extends copyright protection to "computer programs and compilations of data."[3] TRIPS obligates members to comply with the provisions of the Berne Convention for the Protection of Literary and Artistic Works.

TRIPS extends copyright protection to "expressions and not to ideas, procedures, methods of operation or mathematical concepts."[4] Computer programs, whether in source or object code, are to be protected under the agreement to the same extent as literary works. Compilations of data, such as databases or other materials that by reason of their contents constitute "intellectual creations"," are to be protected as copyrighted works.[32]

World Intellectual Property Treaty

The United States participated in the meeting of nations who have joined the World Intellectual Property Organization (WIPO). The WIPO Copyright Treaty[5] was adopted by the Diplomatic Conference on December 20, 1996, and was ratified during the term of the 105th Congress. It was implemented by the Digital Millennium Act.

Rights of Copyright Holders

The WIPO treaty formally extends the rights of copyright holders to information, images, music and software distributed over the Internet.

Protection for Internet Service Providers/Carriers of Electronic Information

The treaty also protects carriers and distributors of electronic information from liability for copyright infringement made by their customers and clients.

Chapter 14 - Highlights of Law Changes and Court Decisions Affecting Education and Libraries

Encyclopedia Brittanica Educational Corp. vs. Crooks 1983

Encyclopedia Brittanica and others sued the Board of Cooperative Educational Services (BOCES) of western New York, a consortium of public school districts, for systematically taping off-air programs that were broadcast on public television stations and making copies available to member schools. The BOCES practice was found not to be fair use and of detrimental effect on the market for the programs produced.

Brussels Satellite Convention - 1984

Prohibits reception of signals from foreign countries that were not specifically beamed at the United States for open reception.

Berne Convention - 1989

1. Effective March 1, 1989. International copyright agreement.
2. No longer requires mandatory copyright notice be placed on works in order to be protected.

Copyright Remedy Clarification Act - 1990

1. Effective November 15, 1990.
2. Makes states and their subsidiary units liable for copyright infringement.

Computer Software Rental Amendments Act of 1990

1. Prohibits the loan or rental of computer software.
2. Provides an exemption for educational institutions or libraries, assuming the software is not limited by licensing agreements and that the programs loaned clearly have on their packaging a copyright warning.

Architectural Works Copyright Protection Act of 1990

Adds plans, drawings and final structure to categories of works protected under copyright.

Basic Books, Inc. vs. Kinko's Graphics Corp. - 1991

A Federal District Court in New York State ruled that Kinko's Graphic Corporation infringed copyrights and didn't exercise fair use, when it photocopied "coursepacks" that included book chapters, and then sold them to students for class work. The court found that Kinko's did not meet most of the fair use factors, especially given Kinko's activities were of a commercial, profit-making nature. Additionally, the court found that the classroom guidelines did not apply to Kinko's. The court did not rule that coursepacks could not constitute fair use in other circumstances.

The Copyright Renewal Act of 1992

1. Provides automatic renewal of works copyrighted between January 1, 1964 and December 31, 1977, for which the copyright holder had not applied for an extension.
2. Provides extension of another 47 years.

The Audio Home Recording Act of 1992

1. All digital audio recorders, except professional models and dictating machines not used to copy music, must contain technology to control serial copying.
2. Provides consumers an exemption for private, non- commercial home recording of analog of analog or digital sound recordings.

Fair Use - 1992

Fair use now applies to unpublished works, as well as published works.

Copyright Reform Act of 1993

1. Eliminates requirement to register with Copyright Office if intending to file lawsuit.
2. No longer required to file to enjoy remedies of statutory damages and attorney's fees.
3. Eliminates Copyright Royalty Tribunal and moves functions into Copyright Office.

Satellite Home Viewer Act of 1994

1. Expanded definition of a cable system to include wireless services.
2. Broadened definition of local service area of primary transmitter.
3. *Prohibits satellite services from carrying local, network programming.
   (* This limitation was modified in later legislation)

Digital Performance Right In Sound Recordings Act 1995

1. Provides copyright owner of a sound recording an exclusive right to perform the recording publicly by means of a digital audio transmission.
2. Primarily aimed at subscription and interactive services.

American Geophysical Union vs. Texaco

Spanning a period from July 1992, until May 1995, a series of court decisions and a final settlement found Texaco in violation of fair use while photocopying articles from periodicals that were registered with the Copyright Clearance Center. (Texaco did not admit to wrongdoing in its settlement) The courts had found that Texaco, as profit-making institution, did not meet the noncommercial nature of the fair use requirements, that it substantially reproduced materials which were often copied to other departments and that the market for the publishers involved was affected since Texaco did not pay royalties to the Copyright Clearance Center.

Texaco agreed to pay settlement and retroactive licensing fee to the CCC. In addition, Texaco agreed to enter into standard license agreements with the CCC during the next five years.

Although a case not directly pertaining to libraries and educational institutions, one of the issues for consideration is the amount being reproduced and how the copied materials are being used in libraries or education.

Legislative Appropriations Act of 1997

1. Permits authorized entity to reproduce or distribute copies of phonorecords of previously

published, non-dramatic literary works, in specialized formats, Exclusively for use by blind or other persons with disabilities.
   a. Excludes standardized, secure or norm referenced tests and related testing material.
   b. Excludes computer programs, except for portions in conventional, human language.

World Intellectual Property Organization Treaty (WIPO)

1. Extends rights of copyright holders to information, images, music and software distributed over the Internet.
2. Protects carriers and distributors of electronic information from liability for copyright infringements made by their customers and clients.
3. Adopted in Diplomatic Conference on December 20, 1996.
4. Implemented in the form of the Digital Millennium Copyright Act.

Sonny Bono Copyright Term Extension Act

1. Public Law No. 105-298 enacted October 27, 1998.
2. Extends the term of copyright protection, for most works, to the life of the author plus 70 years

Digital Millennium Copyright Act

1. Public Law No. 105-304 enacted October 28, 1998.
2. This Act contains four separate acts as listed below.
   a. WIPO Copyright and Performances and Phonograms Treaties Implementation Act - Implemented the WIPO treaty and prohibited circumvention of copyright protection systems and provided protection for copyright management information.
   b. Online Copyright Infringement Liability Limitation Act - Protects carriers and distributors of electronic information from liability for copyright infringements made by their customers and clients.
   c. Computer Maintenance Competition Assurance Act
   d. Vessel Hull Design Protection Act

Digital Theft Deterrence and Copyright Damages Improvement Act of 1999

1. Pub. L. No. 106-160 enacted December 9, 1999.
2. Increased the amount of statutory penalties for copyright violations.

Work Made for Hire and Copyright Corrections Act of 2000

1. Pub. L. No. 106-379 enacted October 27, 2000.
2. Amended the definition of works made for hire.
3. Changed the language regarding Copyright Office fees, and made other technical and conforming amendments to the Copyright Law.

Technology Education, and Copyright Harmonization Act of 2002 (TEACH Act)

1. Division C, Title III, Subtitle C of the 21st Century Department of Justice Appropriations Authorization Act, Public Law No. 107-273 enacted November 2, 2002.
2. Incorporates provisions relating to the use of copyrighted works for distance education.

© IMSI

Appendix A : Copyright Policies

Policy Development

The following statements are recommended for inclusion in developing an institutional copyright policy.

1. That the governing board of the institution intends to abide by the copyright law.

2. That the institution prohibits copying or use of copyrighted material not specifically permitted or exempted by the copyright law.

3. That the institution places the liability for willful infringement upon the person making or requesting a copy or using the material.

4. That the institution creates the position of a copyright officer for the institution. (Does not need to be a new position, but rather the assignment of responsibility)

5. That the institution mandates the development of a copyright manual detailing permissible and restricted activities on the part of the institution's employees.

6. That the institution mandates placement of appropriate warning notices on or near all print, video or computer equipment capable of making or modifying copies.

7. That the institution mandates the development and retention of appropriate copyright records.

Model Copyright Policy # 1

The School Board of (   ), in recognizing the importance of the Copyright Law of the United States (Title 17, United States Code) hereby notifies all employees that a willful infringement of the law may result in disciplinary action.

* Optional Statement

The school board will not provide legal support in such a case where the person has been notified that the potential infringement existed and the individual still has pursued utilizing the materials in such a manner as to result in infringement.

* Use of this statement may be restricted by state laws, local policies or negotiated employee contracts.

Model Copyright Policy # 2

1. School Board employees may use or reproduce copyrighted materials under the provisions of the copyright laws currently in force under Title 17 of the United States Code.

2. Any use or reproduction of copyrighted materials will be done either with the written permission of the copyright holder or within the bounds of "Fair Use" guidelines provided in the Copyright Act, otherwise the individual responsible for use or reproduction may be liable for infringing the copyright under existing laws.

3. The School Board of (   ) in recognizing the importance of the Copyright Law of the United States (Title 17, United States Code) hereby notifies all employees that a willful infringement of the law may result in disciplinary action. In the case of a court action for damages, a finding of willful infringement would preclude the School Board paying any judgment rendered against the employee and paying any attorney's fees or costs which the employee would incur in conjunction with a lawsuit and may render the employee liable to the School Board for any damages which the school Board is liable to pay.

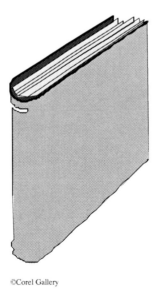

©Corel Gallery

Appendix B : Wording of Copyright Warning Notices

The wording of the copyright warning notices to follow is part of the operational directives of the Copyright Office in Washington. The signs are available commercially from library supply houses and are usually printed in large black letters on yellow poster board background and laminated. The wording is not copyrighted. Any institution could produce their own posters, signs, notices, etc. incorporating the wording.

Warning In A Service Area

The following warning notice conforms to federal directive and should be displayed where orders for photocopying or reproduction services are accepted. It should be displayed so that it is highly visible to patrons requesting services.

NOTICE

Warning Concerning
Copyright Restrictions

The copyright law of the United States (Title 17, United States Code) governs the making of photocopies or other reproductions of copyrighted material.

Under certain conditions specified in the law, libraries and archives are authorized to furnish a photocopy or other reproduction. One of these specified conditions is that the photocopy or reproduction is not to be "used for any purpose other than private study, scholarship or research." If a user makes a request for, or later uses, a photocopy or reproduction for purposes in excess of "Fair Use", that user may be liable for copyright infringement.

This institution reserves the right to refuse to accept a copying order if, in its judgment, fulfillment of the order would involve violation of copyright law.

Warning In A Self-Service Area

This second warning notice should be posted, in a highly visible manner, by each copying machine or device capable of reproducing copyrighted materials that is unattended.

NOTICE

The copyright law of the United States (Title 17, U.S. Code) governs the making of photo copies or other reproductions of copyrighted material. "The person using this equipment is liable for any infringement."

General Warning

The third notice, whose wording is not included specifically in the copyright office directions, is provided as an example of a general statement that may be posted, provided in the form of a handout sheet or affixed to materials with a sticker label.

NOTICE

Computer, CD-ROM, DVD, laserdisc and videocassette programs, audio recordings, books and periodicals are protected by copyright law (Title 17, U.S. Code). Unauthorized use or copying may be prohibited by law.

Appendix C : Sample Permissions Forms

Request for Off Air Taping Within An Institution

This tape was recorded_____on_____ .
                         by myself/at my request   (date)

The 10th consecutive school day from the recording date is_____.
                                                  (date)

I will not use this recording more than once in relevant teaching activities. I will not repeat it more than once for reinforcement.

The 45th day after the recording date will be_____ .
                                             (date)

I understand that I may use this recording from the 11th to the 45th day for teacher evaluation only. It will not be used for student exhibition during this time unless authorization is obtained from the copyright holder.

_____copies have been made of this recording. Each one bears a copy of this statement.

This recording (these recordings) will be_____
                                              erased/destroyed
no later than the 45th day as indicated above.

       Teacher Signature_____

       Media Staff
       Signature _____

RequestTo Duplicate Copyrighted Material

TO:

Date: _____

Firm: _____

Address: _____

_____

FROM:

School/District _____

Department _____

Telephone _____

Person Making Request _____ Title _____

We are requesting authorization to duplicate the following copyrighted material:

Title _____

Author _____

Subject _____

Medium _____

Rationale _____

_____

Number of copies to be made: _____

Copy medium: _____

Use of Copies: _____

Anticipated date of first use: _____

Distribution of copies: _____

****

PRODUCER REPLY:

Permission: ___ granted ___ denied

Details/Restrictions: _____

_____

Signature: _____

Title: _____ Date: _____

Request for Permission To Quote

Dear Sir/Madam:

I am preparing a book/article entitled_____ _____ ,

which will be published by _____ .

It is scheduled to be released _____ .

Attached is a quote I would like to use. The material was taken from pages _____

of _____ by _____ .

The following is the credit line I will use. Please check it for accuracy and make any changes that are necessary.

© 2003 (Insert name of author being quoted)

I would like to request permission to use the quote indicated in my book/article and in all future revisions and editions thereof, including the nonexclusive world rights in all languages. These rights in no way restrict republication of the material by you or those you authorize.

Please sign this form in the appropriate places and return one copy to me in the enclosed stamped envelope. The second copy is for your files.

Should you not control these rights, please let me know the name and address of the person I should contact.

I would appreciate your consideration in granting this request.

Sincerely,

Your Name _____

****
I (We) ___grant) ___deny permission for the use(s) requested above:

Special Conditions: _____

_____

Signature: _____

Title: _____ Date: _____

Signature: _____

Title: _____ Date: _____

Request to Use Rental Video In Classroom

TO:

Date:_____

Rental Source: _____

Address: _____

_____

FROM:

School/District _____

Department _____

Telephone _____

Person Making Request _____Title_____

We are hereby requesting permission to perform the following, copyrighted, rental video program(s) in the classroom **for instructional purposes only!** The programs will be used face-to-face with students, or may be used on a closed circuit system within a school.

Title _____

Title _____

Title _____

Title _____

****

VENDOR REPLY:

Permission: ___ granted ___ denied

Details/Restrictions: _____

_____

Signature: _____

Title: _____ Date: _____

Appendix D : Copyright Office Circulars & Factsheets

Internet and Fax on Demand

The Copyright Office is making some of its more popular circulars and factsheets available via the Internet and fax request. To obtain a document, you may either go to **www.copyright.gov/circs** or call (202) 707-2600. If requesting by FAX, be prepared to provide the document number, which may be found in the far left column of the following, partial index. (A complete index will be provided by the Copyright Office, upon request) Up to three documents will be provided, per FAX request.

Doc. #   Document Title

A-Circulars

101   Copyright Basics (Circ.1)
102   Limitations on Information (Circ. 1b)
103   Publications on Copyright (Circ. 2)
104   Copyright Notice (Circ. 3)
105   Copyright Fees (Circ. 4)
106   Deposit Accounts (Circ. 5)
107   Access/Copies of C.O. Records (Circ. 6)
108   Best Edition (Circ. 7b)
109   Mandatory Deposit (Circ. 7d)
110   Supplementary Registration (Circ. 8)
111   Ideas, Methods, Systems (Circ. 31)
112   Special Handling (Circ. 10)
113   Recordation of Documents (Circ. 12)
114   Derivative Works (Circ. 14)
115   Renewal of Copyright (Circ. 15)
116   Deposit Requirements/VA (Circ. 40a)
117   Extension of Copyright (Circ. 15t)
119   Researching Copyright Status (Circ. 22)
120   Card Catalog/Online Files (Circ. 23)
122   Names, Titles, Short Phrases (Circ. 34)
123   Copyright for Visual Arts (Circ. 40)
124   Duration of Copyright (Circ. 15a)
125   Cartoons/Comic Strips (Circ. 44)
126   Motion Pictures and Videos (Circ. 45)

Doc. #   Document Title

A-Circulars

127	Musical Compositions (Circ. 50)
128	Sound Recordings (Circ. 56)
129	Music/Sound Recordings (Circ. 56a)
130	Computer Programs (Circ. 61)
131	Serials (Circ. 62)
132	Daily Newspapers (Circ. 62b)
134	Secure Tests (Circ. 64)
135	Databases (Circ. 65)
136	International Copyright (Circ. 38a)
137	Works-Made-For-Hire (Circ. 9)
138	Effects of Not Replying (Circ. 7c)
139	Architectural Works (Circ. 41)
140	Multimedia Works (Circ. 55) 5
141	Highlights/GATT/VRAA (Circ. 38b)
145	Computing/Measuring Devices (Circ. 33)
147	Online Works (Circ. 66)

B-Regulations/Announcements

201	GATT Regulation (ML-509)

C-Other Copyright Publications

301	Have a "?"/Before You Call (SL9)

Glossary

A

Aggregate, In the - The total amount of copyrighted material taken from a single, copyrighted work.

Audiovisual Works - Works that consist of a series of related images which are intrinsically intended to be shown by the use of machines or devices such as projectors, viewers, or electronic equipment, together with accompanying sounds if any, regardless of the nature of the material objects, such as films or tapes, in which they are embodied.

C

Collective Work - Is a work, such as a periodical issue, anthology, or encyclopedia, in which a number of contributions, constituting separate and independent works in themselves, are assembled into a collective whole.

Compilation - Is a work formed by the collection and assembling of preexisting materials or of data that are selected, coordinated, or arranged in such a way that the resulting work, as a whole, constitutes an original work of authorship. The term "compilation" includes collective works.

Computer Program - Is a set of statements or instructions to be used directly or indirectly in a computer in order to bring about a certain result.

Copies - Are material objects, other than phonorecords, in which a work is fixed by any method now known or later developed, and from which the work can be perceived, reproduced, or otherwise communicated, either directly or the with the aid of a machine or device. The term "copies" includes the material object, other than a phonorecord, in which the work is first fixed. (**See Fixed**)

D

Derivative Work - Is a work based upon one or more preexisting works, such as a translation, musical arrangement, dramatization, fictionalization, motion picture version, sound recording, art reproduction, abridgment, condensation, or any other form in which a work may be recast, transformed, or adapted. A work consisting of editorial revisions, annotations, elaborations, or other modifications which, as a whole, represent an original work of authorship is a derivative work.

Display - To display a work means to show a copy of it, either directly or by means of a film, slide, television image, or any other device or process, or, in the case of a motion picture or other audiovisual work, to show individual images nonsequentially.

Dramatic Work - A work in which there is a plot depicted by action.

E

Educational Institutions - Nonprofit organizations whose primary focus is supporting research and instructional activities of educators and students for noncommercial purposes.

Educators - Faculty, teachers, instructors and others who engage in scholarly, research and instructional activities for educational institutions.

F

Fixed - A work is "fixed" in a tangible medium of expression when its embodiment in a copy or phonorecord, by or under the authority of the author, is sufficiently permanent or stable to permit it to be perceived, reproduced, or otherwise communicated for a period of more than transitory duration. A work consisting of sounds, images or both, that are transmitted, is "fixed" for purposes of this title if a fixation of the work is being made simultaneously with its transmission.

I

In the Aggregate - (See Aggregate, In the)

L

Literary Works - Are works , other than audiovisual works, expressed in words, numbers, or other verbal or numerical symbols or indicia, regardless of the nature of the material objects, such as books, periodicals, manuscripts, phonorecords, film, tapes, disks, or cards in which they are embodied.

M

Motion Pictures - Are audiovisual works consisting of a series of related images which, when shown in succession, impart an impression of motion, together with accompanying sounds, if any.

N

Non-Dramatic Work - A work that does not contain a plot depicted by action.

P

Perform - To perform a work means to recite, render, play, dance, or act it, either directly or by means of any device or process, or, in the case of a motion picture or other audiovisual work, to show the images in any sequence or to make the sounds accompanying it audible.

Performance, Dramatic - Any opera, operetta, musical, comedy, play or like production in which there is a plot depicted by action. (**See Dramatic Work**)

Performance, Non-Dramatic - Documentaries, readings from a book, musical compositions or any performance that does not involve a plot depicted by action. (**See Non-Dramatic Work**)

Performance, Public - To perform or display a work "publicly" means:
(1)   to perform or display it at a place open to the public or at any place where a substantial number of persons outside of a normal circle of a family and its social acquaintances is gathered; or
(2)   to transmit or otherwise communicate a performance or display of the work to a place specified by clause (1) or to the public, by means of any device or process, whether the members of the public capable of receiving the performance or display receive it in the same place or in separate places and at the same time or at different times.

Phonorecords - Are material objects in which sounds, other than those accompanying a motion picture or other audiovisual work, are fixed by any method now known or later developed, and from which the sounds can be perceived, reproduced, or otherwise communicated, either directly or with the aid of a machine or device. The term "phonorecords" includes the material object in which the sounds are first fixed.

Public Performance - See Performance, Public

T

Transmit - To "transmit" a performance or display is to communicate it by any device or process whereby images or sounds are received beyond the place from which they are sent.

Reference Citations

Quick Reference Section

1. # 17, USC, Section 102(a)
2. # 17, USC, Section 106
3. # 17, USC, Section 504(c)(1)(2)

Chapter 1 - Items Protected/Not Protected

1. US Constitution, Article I, Section 8, Clause 8

Chapter 2 - Fair Use

1. Berlin vs. E.C. Publications, Inc.; Elsmere Music, Inc. vs. National Broadcasting Company.
2. Italian Book Corp. vs. American Broadcasting Cos.

Chapter 3 - Photocopying

1. House Report No. 94-1476, p. 68-70
2. # 17, USC, Section 108
3. American Association of University Professor's Bulletin, September, 1978, by John C. Stedman, emeritus professor of law, University of Wisconsin at Madison.
4. House Conference Report, No. 94-1733, p. 72-74

Chapter 4 - Public Performance

1. # 17, USC, Section 101 (definition of "perform")
2. # 17, USC, Section 101
3. # 17, USC, Section 110(1)
4. House Report, p. 82
5. House Report, p. 81
6. Ibid.
7. House Report, p. 82
8. # 17, USC, Section 110(4)

Chapter 5 - Music

1. House Report, p. 71
2. Althouse, Jay, Copyright: The Complete Guide for Music Educators. Music In Action, East Stroudsburg, PA: 1984, p. 51; 54.

Chapter 7 - Video

1. Congressional Record, October 14, 1981.
2. Senate Report No. 94-473, p. 65-66.
3. Congressional Record-House, Vol. 122, No. 144, (Sept. 22, 1976), p. H10875.
4. Mr. James Bouras, Vice-President, Secretary & Deputy Attorney,
   Motion Picture Association of America, Inc., 522 Fifth Avenue, N.Y., N.Y. 10036.
   (212) 840-6161
5. # 17, USC, Section 110(2)
6. # 17, USC, Section 112(b)

Chapter 8 - Computer Software

1. CONTU Final Report, July 31, 1978, p. 12

Chapter 9 - Guidelines for Educational Multi-Media

1. Fair Use Guidelines for Educational Multi-Media.

Chapter 11 - The Internet and Distance Learning

1. *The National Law Journal*, May 20, 1996. "Net Users, Could Face IP Liability." Christopher Wolf, p. C35.

Chapter 13 - International Copyright

1. Sec. 804(c) of the Computer Software Rental Amendments Act of 1990, incoporated into 17 U.S.C. 109(b)(1)(A)
2. Agreement on Trade Related Aspects of Intellectual Property Rights, GATT document MTN/FA II-AIC (1994) referred to as TRIPS Agreement, Part II, Article 11.
3. TRIPS agreement, supra, part 2, article 10.
4. TRIPS agreement, supra, part 2, article 9.
5. TRIPS agreement, supra, part 2, article 12.

Bibliography

Books andArticles

Althouse, Jay. *Copyright: The Complete Guide for Music Educators*. East Stroudsburg, PA: Music In Action, 1984.

Althouse, Jay. *Copyright: The Complete Guide for Music Educators, 2nd Edition*. Van Nuys, CA: Alfred Publising Company, Inc., 1997.

Bender, Ivan R. Public Libraries and Copyright. *Television Licensing Guide*, Vol. 7, No. 6, March, 1987.

Bielefield, Arlene. *Technology and Copyright Law: A Guidebook for the Library, Research and Teaching Professions*. New York,NY: Neal-Schuman Publishers, Inc., 1997.

Botterbusch, Hope Roland. *Copyright in the Age of New Technology*. Bloomington, IN: Phi Delta Kappa Educational Foundation, 1996.

Brinson, J. and Radcliffe, M. *Multimedia Law Handbook: A Practical Guide for Developers*. Menlo Park: CA: Ladera Press, 1994.

Bruwelheide, Janice. The Copyright Primer for Educators and Librarians. Chicago,IL: American Library Associaton, 1995.

Crews, Kenneth D. *Copyright Essentials for Librarians and Educators*. Indiana University - Purdue University, 1999.

Congressional Record - House, Vol 122, No. 144, (Sept. 22, 1976), p. H10875.

Copyrights Act. 17 U.S. Code. 1976. Public Law 94-553.

"Copyright & You". On-going column in *Tech Trends*. Washington, DC: Association for Educational Communications and Technology.

Copyright Law Revision. House Report 94-1476, 1976.

Copyright Law Revision. Senate Report 94-473, 1976.

Copyright Law Revision. Conference Report 94-1733, 1976.

Faoborg, Karen. The Music Educator's Guide to Copyright Law. *The American Music Teacher*, 36:22-3, S/O, 1986.

Final Report of the National Commission On New Technological Uses of Copyrighted Works. Washington, D.C.: Library of Congress, 1979.

Gasaway, Laura N. and Sarah K. Wiant. *Libraries and Copyright: A Guide to Copyright Law in the 1990's*. Washington,DC: Special Libraries Association, 1994.

Gasaway, Laura N. ed. Growing Pains: Adapting Copyright for Libraries, Education and Society. Littleton: Fred B. Rothman and Co., 1997.

General Guide to the Copyright Act of 1976. Washington, D.C.: Copyright Office, Library of Congress, 1977.

Helm, Virginia M. *What Educators Should Know About Copyright*. Bloomington, IN: Phi Delta Kappa Educational Foundation, 1986.

Henn, Harry G. *Henn on Copyright Law*. Practising Law Institute, 1991.

Johnston, Donald F. *The Copyright Handbook, 2nd. Ed*. New York: R.R. Bowker Company, 1982.

Kreamer, Jean T., et.al. Video and Copyright: An Overview of Some Basic Issues. *Sightlines*, Vol. 22, No. 4, Fall 1989.

Lehman, Bruce A. Intellectual Property and the National Information Infrastructure: A Preliminary Draft of the Report on the Working Group on Intellectual Property Rights. Washington, DC: July, 1994. (www.uspto.gov/text/pto/nii/ipwg.html)

Miller, Jerome K. *Using Copyrighted Videocassettes in Classrooms, Libraries And Training Centers*. Friday Harbor, WA: Copyright Information Services, 1988.

Miller, Jerome K. *The Copyright Directory*. Friday Harbor, WA: Copyright Information Services, 1984.

Miller, Jerome K. *Video Copyright Permissions: A Guide To Securing Permission To Retain, Perform, And Transmit Television Programs Videotaped Off The Air*. Friday Harbor, WA: Copyright Information Services, 1989.

National Commission on New Technological Uses of Copyrighted Works (CONTU). *Final Report of the National Commission on New Technological Uses of Copyrighted Works, July 31, 1978*. Washington, DC: Library of Congress, 1979.

National Conference on Educational Fair Access and the New Media. *What's Fair?: A Report on the Proceedings of the National Conference on Educational Fair Access and the New Media.* Bloomington, IN: TECHNOS Press, 1994.

The Official Fair-Use Guidelines: Complete Texts of Four Official Documents Arranged for *Use by Educators.* Friday Harbor, WA: Copyright Information Services, 1985.

Patry, William F. and George, Vicky A., Ed. United States Adheres to the Berne Convention. *Journal of the Copyright Society of the USA.*, 36, No. 1, October 1988, p. 1-80.

Patry, Willam F. *The Fair Use Privilege in Copyright Law.* Bureau of National Affairs, 1985.

Patterson, L.R. & Lindberg, S.W. *The Nature of Copyright: A Law of User's Rights.* Athens, GA: University of Georgia Press, 1991.

Pitman, Randy. Video In Libraries 1988: A Review. *Video Librarian*, Vol. 3, No. 11, February 1989.

Rose, Lance. *Netlaw: Your Rights In the Online World.* Berkeley, CA: Osborne McGraw-Hill, 1995.

Seltzer, Leon E. *Exemptions and Fair Use In Copyright.* Cambridge, MA: Harvard University Press, 1978.

Shemel, Sidney and Krasilovsky, M. William. *This Business of Music.* New York: Billboard Publications, 1985.

Simpson, Carol Mann. *Copyright for School Libraries:A Practical Guide.* Worthington,OH: Linworth Publishing,Inc., 1994.

Simpson, Carol Mann. *Copyright for Schools: A Practical Guide.* Worthington,OH: Linworth Publishing,Inc., 1997.

Sinofsky, Esther R. *Off-Air Videotaping in Education: Copyright Issues, Decisions, Implications.* New York: R.R. Bowker Company, 1984.

Sinofsky, Esther R. *A Copyright Primer for Educational and Industrial Media Producers.* Friday Harbor, WA: Copyright Information Services, 1988.

Stim, Richard. Getting Permission: How to License and Clear Copyrighted Materials Online and Off. Berkeley, CA: Nolo Press, 2000.

Strong, William S. *The Copyright Book: A Practical Guide.* Cambridge, MA: MIT Press, 1992.

Talab, R.S. *Copyright and Instructional Technologies; A Guide to Fair Use and Permissions Procedures.* Washington, D.C.: Association for Educational Communications and Technology, 1989.

The United States Copyright Law: A Guide for Music Educators. Arlington, VA: Music Educators National Conference, Music Publishers' Association of the United States, Music Teachers National Association, National Music Publishers' Association and the National Association of Schools of Music. (Not copyrighted. Publishing date not indicated.)

Vlcek, Dr. Charles W. *Copyright Policy Development: A Resource Book For Educators.* Friday Harbor, WA: Copyright Information Services, 1987. (Now distributed by AECT)

Vlcek, Dr. Charles W. *Adoptable Copyright Policy.* AECT, 1992.

Weil, Ben H. and Polansky, Barbara F. *Modern Copyright Fundamentals.* Medford, NJ: Learned Information, Inc., 1989.

Young, Woody. © *Copyright Law: What You Don't Know Can Co$t You!* San Juan Capistrano, CA: Jay Publishing, 1988.

Internet Resources

A Guide for Music Educators

www.menc.org

[In heading, click on "Index" then scroll alphabetically to "C" section for "Copyright Information" and for "Copyright Law: A Guide for Music Educators"]

Center for Democracy and Technology.

Makes available information on copyright protection and related legislation.

(http://www.cdt.org)

Copyright Act, USC TITLE 17 - (Cornell)

http://www4.law.cornell.edu/uscode/17/

Copyright and Intellectual Property Resources

International Federation of Libraries.

http://www.ifla.org/II/cpyright.htm

Copyright for Music Librarians

www.lib.jmu.edu/org/mla

Copyright Management Center (U.of Texas)

http://www.utsystem.edu/OGC/IntellectualProperty/cprtindx.htm"

Copyright Resources On-Line

http://www.library.yale.edu/~okerson/copyproj.html

Copyright Sites (Penn State)

http://www.libraries.psu.edu/mtss/copyright.html

Fair Use

http://fairuse.stanford.edu/

Fair Use: Library Copyright Guidlines (Stanford)

http://fairuse.stanford.edu/library/index.html

Fair Use and Higher Education

http://www.iupui.edu

Fair Use Guidelines for Educational Multimedia (Penn State)

http://www.libraries.psu.edu/mtss/fairuse/guidelines.html

Guidelines for the Use of Music Under Copyright
http://www.reach.net/~scherer/p/copyhelp.htm

Library of Congress Home Page

See section entitled "Thomas" for up-to-date reporting on status of proposed copyright legislation.

http://lcweb.loc.gov/

U.S. Copyright Office Home Page

http://lcweb.loc.gov/copyright/

WWW Virtual Library: Intellectual Property Law

http://www.law.indiana.edu/v-lib/

Associations Providing Copyright Information

American Library Association
50 East Huron Street
Chicago, IL 60611
(800) 545-2433
FAX: (312) 440-9374
www.ala.org

Provides publications.

Association for Educational Communications and Technology
1800 North Stonelake Dr., Suite 2
Bloomington, IN 47408
(877) 347-7834
www.aect.org

Provides publications.

Association for Information Media and Equipment (AIME)
P.O. Box 9844
Cedar Rapids, IA 52409-9844
(319) 654-0608
FAX: (319) 654-0609
www.aime.org

Provides a videotape, information packet and copyright hotline free for members. May purchase videotape and packet even if not a member. For information, call **(800) 444-4203**.

Discovery Communications, Inc., Dept. CIC
7700 Wisconsin Avenue
Bethesda, MD 20814
(301) 986-1999
www.discovery.com

Provides a free12 page guide, "All About Copyright," which deals with off-air videotaping.

Software & Information Industry Association (Formely Software Publishers Association)
1730 M Street, Northwest
Suite 700
Washington, DC 20036-4510
(202) 4521600
FAX: (202) 223-8756
www.siia.net

Provides a hotline, **(800) 388-7478**, to report acts of software piracy. Provides a videotape, self-audit kit and other useful information, including data on recent court cases, number of calls to the hotline each month and number of cease and desist letters they have sent.

United States Copyright Office

Copyright Office
Library of Congress
Washington DC 20559-6000
(202) 707-3000
www.copyright.gov

Information specialist available, M-F, 8:30-5:00, ET. Questions are answered, however, the Copyright Office does not provide interpretations or respond to whether a specific circumstance may be potentially in violation of the law.

Request Publications/Applications

May find forms and publications at Copyright Office website, may request publications and application forms 24hrs./day at **(202) 707-9100,** or mail a request to:

Reference and Bibliography Section, LM-451
Copyright Office
Library of Congress
Washington, DC 20559

Conducting Searches

Searches for the status of copyright on materials that one may desire to utilize may be performed on-line. Directions may be found at the Copyright Office Web Site. Requests to have staff of the Copyright Office conduct a search may also be made. A fee is involved for conducting such searches and an additional fee, per search item, if it is desired to have the search certified. Search requests should be made to the following address:

Library of Congress
Copyright Office
Reference and Bibliography Section, LM-451
101 Independence Avenue, S.E.
Washington, DC 20559-6000
(202) 707-6850

Copyright Cleared Production Music Libraries

(Theme, background, special effect)

The following sources provide music in the form of tapes or compact discs that may be used to accompany media presentations and productions of all types. The cost structures vary as some charge on the basis of the music actually used and others outright sell their music libraries, granting permission for use, under specific conditions. This list and the lists of other sources that follow are provided for information purposes only and do not constitute an endorsement.

Companies, preceded by an asterisk (*), are often found in listings of resources used in productions by educational institutions.

Aircraft Production Music Libraries
162 Columbus Avenue
Boston, MA 02116
(800) 343-2514
FAX: (617) 303-7666
www.aircraftmusiclibrary.com

*Award Winning Music
711 Medford Center, Suite 353
Medford, OR 97504
(800) 716-0065
FAX: (703) 991-8382
www.royaltyfreemusic.com

BBC Sound Effects Library
c/o Films for the Humanities, Inc.
12 Perrine Road
Monmouth JCT, NJ 08852-2730
(609) 275-1400
www.films.com

Corelli-Jacobs Recording, Inc.
25 W. 45th Street
New York, NY 10036-4902
(212) 382-0220
FAX: (212) 382-0278

*DeWolfe Music Library, Inc.
25 West 45th Street
New York, NY 10036-4902
(800) 221-6713 or (212) 382-0220
FAX: (212) 382-0278
www.dewolfemusic.com

Don Elliott Productions
15 Bridge Road
Weston, CT 06883-2539
(203) 226-4200

First Com Music
1325 Capital Parkway, Suite 109
Dallas, TX 75006
(800) 858-8880
www.firstcom.com

*Fresh - The Music Library
34 S. Main Street
Hanover, NH 03755
(800) 545-0688
FAX: (603) 643-1388
www.freshmusic.com

*Network Music, Inc.
15150 Avenue of Science
San Diego, CA 92128-3416
(858) 451-6400
(800) 854-2075
FAX: (858) 457-6409
www.networkmusic.com

Omnimusic Production Music Library.
52 Main Street
Port Washington, NY 11050
(800) 828-6664
FAX: (516) 883-0271
www.omnimusic.com

*Promusic, Inc.
941A Clint Moore Road

Boca Raton, FL 33487
(561) 995-0331
(800) 322-7879
FAX: (561) 995-8434
www.promusic-inc.com

Sear Sound Recording
353 W. 48th Street
New York, NY 10036-1324
(212) 582-5380

Signature Music Library
P.O. Box 921
Chesterton, IN 46304-0921
(219) 921-0205
(800) 888-7151
FAX: 419-844-2891
www.sigmusic.com

*Soper Sound Music Library
P.O. Box 869
Ashland, OR 97520
(800) 227-9980
(541) 552-0830
FAX: (541) 552-0832
www.sopersound.com

Sound dogs.com, Inc.
P.O. Box 5021
Santa Monica, CA 90409-5021
(877) 315-3647
www.sounddogs.com

Soundfx.com
N.R.G. Concepts, Inc.
500 N. Citrus Avenue
Coving, CA 91723
(888) 826-5855
E-mail: info@soundfx.com
www.soundfx.com

Sound Hound, Inc.
45 West 45th Street
New York, NY 10036-4602
(212) 575-8664

Sound Ideas
105 West Beaver Creek Road
Suite 4
Richmond Hill, Ontario Canada L4B 1 C6
(800) 387-3030
E-mail: info@sound-ideas.com
www.sound-ideas.com

*Soundzabound Music Library, LL.C.
P.O. Box 492199
Atlanta, GA 30349-2199
(888) 834-1792
(770) 461-7018
www.soundzabound.com
Southern Music Publishing Co., Inc.
810 7th Avenue
New York, NY 10019-5818
(212) 265-3910
FAX: (212) 489-2465

*Valentino Production Music, Inc.
500 Executive Boulevard
Elmsford, NY 10523-0534
(914) 347-7878
FAX: (212) 347-4764
www.tvmusic.com

Zelman Studios, Ltd.
623 Cortelyou Road
Brooklyn, NY 11218-4803
(718) 941-5500

Public Domain Music

The following is a reference site that assists in identifying music and songs that are in the public Domain.

Haven Sound, Inc. Public Domain Music. February, 2003.
www.pdinfo.com/list/g.htm

Sources For ClipArt

Electronic Clip Art, General (Computer Clip Art)

Adobe Systems, Inc.
345 Park Avenue
San Jose, CA 95110-2704
(800) 833-6687
(415) 961-4400
www.adobe.com
For: PC/Mac

Corel Corporation
1600 Carlilng Avenue
Ottawa, Ontario Canada K1Z8R7
(800) 772-6735
www.corel.com
For: PC/Mac

Dream Maker Software
925 W. Kenyon Avenue, #16
Englewood, CO 80110-3473
(303) 762-1001
FAX: (303) 362-0762
For: PC/Mac

Dynamic Graphics, Inc.
6000 N. Forest Park Drive
P.O. Box 1901
Peoria, IL 61614-3592
(800) 255-8800
FAX: (309) 688-5873
Email: service@creatas.com
www.creatas.com

ImageBuilder Software
8840 Southwest Burnham Street
Portland, OR 97223
(503) 684-5151
FAX: (503) 639-6334

Imageline, Inc.
10384 Leadbetter Road
Ashland, VA 23005
(804) 550-7650

Macromedia, Inc.
600 Townsend Street
San Francisco, CA 94103-4945
(800) 288-4797
(415) 252-2000
FAX: (415) 626-0554
www.macromedia.com

Medina Software, Inc.
385 Commerce Way
Longwood, FL 32750-7637
(407) 260-1676

Nova Development Corporation
23801 Calabasas Rd., Suite 2005
Calabasas, CA 91302-1547
(818) 591-9600
FAX: (818) 591-8885
E-mail: custsuc@novadevelopment.com
www.novadevelopment.com

Electronic Clip Art For Education (Mostly Free)

About Secondary School Educators
[Teacher clip art for grades 7-12]
http://7-12educators.miningco.com/cs/
teacherclipart

Discovery School's Clip Art Gallery
http://school.discovery.com/clipart/index.html

Educational Cyber Playground
[Listing and links to several free sites containing graphics oriented toward education]
www.edu-cyberpg.com

EyeWire
www.eyewire.com

Free Clip Art
www.free-clip-art.com

Imaages on the Web - Skyline College Library
[URL links to a number of digital image sources useful for K-12, college, university and public libraries. Includes specialized, graphic search engines]
http://skylinecollege.net/library/imagelinks.html

Microsoft Design Gallery Live
http://dgl.microsoft.com
Teacher Files.Com
www.teacherfiles.com/clip_art.htm

Teaching.Com
[Provides listing of URL's for various sources of clip art, photos, animated GIF's, etc.]
www.teaching.com/ednow/resources.cfm?ID=25

Teachnet.Com
www.teachnet.com/how_to/clipart

Teach-Nology - The Web Portal for Educators
[Large listing of web tools for educators, including clip art]
http://teachers.teach-nology.com/web_tools/web_site/clip_art

Licensing/Performance Rights Agencies/Societies

Non-Dramatic Musical Works

The following organizations provide licensing arrangements for the performance of non-dramatic, musical works:
American Society of Composers, Authors and Publishers (ASCAP)

One Lincoln Plaza
New York, New York 10023-7129
(212) 595-3050
www.ascap.com

Broadcast Music, Inc. (BMI)
320 West 57th Street
New York, New York 10019-3790
(212) 586-2000
FAX: (212) 956-2059
www.bmi.com

Society of European Stage Authors & Composers, Inc. (SESAC)
152 W. 57th Street, 57th Fl
New York, New York 10019
(212) 586-3450
FAX: (212) 489-5699
www.sesac.com

Dramatic & Dramitico-Musical Works (Musicals, Plays)

The following organizations provide licensing arrangements for the performance of dramatico-musical works: (Plays and Play Brokers)

Tams-Witmark Music Library, Inc.
560 Lexington Avenue, FL 12
New York, New York 10017
(212) 688-9191
FAX: (212) 688-5656
www.trans-witmark.com

Rodgers & Hammerstein Library
1065 Avenue of the Americas
New York, New York 10018
(917) 510-0110
www.rnh.com

Music Theatre International
421 West 54th Street
New York, New York 10019
(212) 541-4684

FAX: (212) 397-4684
www.mtishows.com

Playbill, Inc.
3715 61st Street
Woodside, NY 11377-2593
(718) 335-4033

Samuel French, Inc.
45 West 25th Street, Dept. W
New York, New York 10010-2751
(212) 206-8990
FAX: (212) 206-1429
www.samuelfrench.com

Recording Rights

The following agency handles recording rights for most music publishers. Such rights would include recording copyrighted music for use as a sound track on a video or multi-media production.

The Harry Fox Agency
711 3rd Avenue
New York, New York 10017
(212) 370-5330
FAX: 212-953-2384
www.nmpa.org

Non-Instructional Video Performances (Public Performance Rights)

The following agencies provide public performance rights for non-profit groups, government organizations, schools and libraries:

The Motion Picture Licensing Corporation
5455 Centinela Avenue
Los Angeles, CA 90066-6970

(800) 462-8855
(310) 822-4440
www.mplc.com

Movie Licensing USA
201 South Jefferson Avenue
St. Louis, MO 63103-2579
(877) 321-1300 (K-12 Public Schools)
(888) 267-2658 (Public Libraries)
FAX: (877) 876-9873
www.movlic.com

Reproduction Rights for Print Documents Distributed On and Off-line

The Copyright Clearance Center (CCC)
222 Rosewood Drive
Danvers, MA 01923
(978) 646-8600
www.copyright.com

Index

A

Admission Charge
  performance, public   **23**
After School Programs
  use of videos   **45**
American Geophysical Union vs. Texaco   **84**
Architectural Works Copyright Protection Act   **83**
Archival Backup
  audio cassettes   **27**
Archival Copy
  computer software   **47**, **53**
ASCAP   **95**
Associations
  providing copyright information   **107**
Audio Cassettes
  archival backup   **27**
Audiovisual Works
  audio cassettes
    archival backup   **27**
  changing formats   **28**
  duplication
    for deaf and blind   **27**
  filmstrips
    salvaging damaged   **27**
  multi-media productions, use in   **60**
  permissible uses   **27**
  photographs
    copying   **28**
  photographs, drawings, charts   **27**
  prohibitions   **27**
Authors Rights. *See Rights, Authors*

B

Basic Books, Inc. vs. Kinko's Graphics Corp. -
  199   **83**
Berne Convention
  registration requirement   **80**
  U.S. Copyright Law, impact on   **78–79**
  works protected under   **79**
Big Books   **19**
Black-line Masters   **20**
BMI   **77**, **95**
Books
  recording from   **28**
Broadcasting, Instructional   **35**
Brussels Satellite Convention   **82**
Burlesque

fair use   **11**

C

Cable
  recording from   **32**
  recording from by students   **43**
  using music on   **45**
Cartoon Characters
  using   **29**
Cartoon characters
  copying   **29**
CD-ROM
  copying from   **66**, **67**
  networking   **66**, **67**
Charts   **27**
Citing Resources
  electronic media
    bibliographic format   **69**
Classroom
  big books   **19**
  black-line masters   **20**
  cable
    taping from by students   **43**
  clip art
    sources for   **112**
  computer software
    donations, use of   **55**
  consumable works   **14**
  current news articles   **20**
  ditto master   **20**
  donations
    computer software, installation of   **55**
  off-air taping
    10 day use, student absence   **44**
  performance, public   **21**
  photocopying
    multiple copies   **13–14**
    single copies   **13**
  video programs
    foreign, use of   **43**
    home use vs. school use versions   **44**
    PTA purchased, use of   **43**
  videocassettes
    closed circuit TV, use on   **4**, **33**
    foreign, use of   **43**
    home use only, use of purchased   **3**, **34**
    home use only, use of rental   **3**, **34**
    PTA purchased, use of   **43**
    use by community members   **41**
    use by parents   **41**
    use of, general   **38**
Clip Art
  for education   **112**

sources for **112**
student newspaper, use in **52**
Closed Circuit TV
use of **4**
video programs, use on **42**
videocassettes, use on **4**, **42**
Computer Software. *See also Berne Convention*; *International Copyright*
archival copy **47**, **53**
changing format **48**
copying portions **54**
creating works
based on other's content **55**
databases
copying from **49**, **53**
creation and distribution of **50**, **55**
donations
installation of **55**
use of **55**
duplication of **47**, **51**
hard disk
transferring programs to **48**
installing personally owned **55**
lab pack
duplication of **53**
making backups for **51**
multiple machine loading **49**
networking **49**, **52**
personally owned
installing **55**
Computer Software Rental Amendments Act of 1990 **83**
Consumable Works
reproduction of **14**
Contracts. *See Licensing*; *Purchase Agreements*
CONTU **49**
Converting
records
to tape or CD **29**
Copying
cartoon characters **29**
from the Internet **74**
photographs **28**
Copyright Information
associations providing **107**
Internet resources **105**
Copyright Law
changes affecting education & libraries **82**, **83**, **84**
Copyright Notice
mandatory requirement **79**
Copyright Office
address **6**, **18**, **108**
FAX documents, on request **95**

home page **106**, **107**
searches, requesting from **75**
Copyright Reform Act of 1993 **84**
Copyright Remedy Clarification Act - 1990 **82**
Copyright Status. *See Searches: copyright status of works*

D

Databases
copying from **49**
creation and distribution of **50**, **55**
screen capture from **53**
using data in
multi-media productions **61**
Definitions **97**
Digital Millennium Copyright Act **85**
Digital Performance Right In Sound Recordings Act **84**
Digital Special Effects
use of **42**
Digital Theft Deterrence Act **85**
Digitized Images
use in multi-media productions **63**
Digitizing
video
placing on server **44**
Distance Learning **70–72**
activities not permitted **6–7**, **71–72**
activities permitted **6**, **71–72**
copyrighted works, use of **70–72**
photographs, charts, tables
display of **74**
Donations
computer software
installation of **55**
use of **55**
videocassette programs
use of **38**
Drawings **27**
Duplication
audiovisual works
for deaf and blind **27**

E

E-mail
magazine articles
permissibility of forwarding **73**
messages
permissibility of forwarding **73**
Education
changes in law, affecting **82**
Electronic Media
citing resources **69**

Employees
  and web site ownership **70**
Encyclopedia Brittanica Educational Corp. vs.
    Croo **82**
Entertainment
  videocassettes, use of **41**

F

Facsimile (FAX) Reproduction **18**, **19**
Fair Use
  criteria for **10**
  functional test **11**
  incidental reproduction **11**
  other Applications **11**
  satire, burlesque & parody **11**
Fair Use - 1992 **83**
Fax Copying **18**, **19**
Filmstrips **27**
  salvaging damaged **27**
Foreign Programs
  video, use of **43**
Formats
  changing **28**

G

GATT Agreement
  U.S. Copyright Law, impact on **80**
  works protected **80**
Glossary **97**
Graphics
  Internet
    copying from **74**
    posting to **74**

H

Handicapped
  recording of
    transmissions **38**
Home Use Only Video Programs
  vs. school use videos
    use in classroom **44**
Home Use Only Videocassettes
  closed circuit TV, use on **4**
  licensing
    for library performance **35**
    for school performance **35**
  purchase and use **3**, **34**
  rental and use **3**, **34**, **39**
  vs. school use videos
    use in classroom **44**

I

Illustrations
  multi-media productions
    use in **60**
Instructional Transmissions
  recording of **37**
Interlibrary Loan **17**
International Copyright **78**, **78–79**
  registration requirement **80**
  U.S. Copyright law, impact on **78–79**
Internet. *See also Multi-Media Productions*
  citing resources
    bibliographic format **69**
  copying from **74**
  copyright information
    on-line **105**
  downloading news articles **72**
  graphics
    copying **74**
    posting **74**
  linking
    legality **69**
  providers, copyright protection for **81**
  using material from **69**

L

Laserdiscs
  copying from **67**
  use of **67**
Legislative Appropriations Act of 1997 **84**
Liability
  under Copyright Law **1**
Library
  CD-ROM
    copying from **67**
    networking **67**
  changes in law, affecting **82**
  databases
    creation and distribution of **50**, **55**
  fax copying **19**
  laserdiscs
    copying from **67**
    use of **67**
  licensing videos
    for performance in **35**
  performance, public **22**
  photocopying
    interlibrary loan **17**
    reserve use **16**
    systematic reproduction **15**
  public performance rights **22**
  reserves

digital **51**
video programs
use of **34**
videocassettes
use of **34**
warning notices. *See Warning Notices, Copyright*
Licensing **76**
videos
for performance in libraries **35**
for performance in schools **35**
Licensing Agencies **77**, **113**
Linking Websites
legality **69**
Lyrics
music
editing **24**
parody **25**

M

Magazine Articles
permissibility of
posting on web site **73**
permissibility of e-mailing **73**
Maps
tracing **27**
Multi-Media Productions
alterations to original, copyrighted works **63**
citing sources requirement **62**
duplications beyond specified limits **63**
Internet, using materials from **62**
limitations, copying and distribution **61**
permission, when still required **61**
permitted uses by educators **58**
permitted uses by students **57**
portion limitations **59**
from illustrations and photographs **60**
from motion media **60**
from music, lyrics and music video **60**
from numerical data sets **61**
from text material **60**
preparation by educators **57**
preparation by students **57**
time limits on use of **59**
use of digitized images **63**
use of scanned images **63**
use restrictions, notifying others **62**
Multiple Machine Loading
computer software **49**
Music
arrangements **25**
cable
use on **45**

copyright cleared
sources of **110**
editing **24**, **26**, **43**
lyrics
editing **24**
multi-media productions
use in **60**
performance, public **23**
license **95**
permissible uses **24**
photocopying **26**
sheet music **24**
prohibitions on use **25**
public domain **111**
recording **24**
selling copies **25**
reproduction **24**
royalties **25**
Music Libraries
copyright cleared
sources of **110**

N

Narrating
recording stories
for the legally blind **28**
Networking
computer software **49**, **52**
News Articles, Current
downloading from Web **72**
photocopying **20**
Newspaper, Student
use of clip art **52**

O

Off-Air Taping
10 day use
student absence **44**
at home for school use **32**
closed circuit TV, use on **4**, **33**
for classroom use **3**
for deaf & hearing impaired **31**
from cable or satellite **3**, **32**
from satellite **42**
retaining of tape **31**
sources from which to **30**
use period **30**
Out-of-Print
materials **20**
reproducing **20**
searches **75**

P

Parody
  fair use   **11**
  lyrics   **25**
Patent Law   **9**
Penalties
  under Copyright Law   **1**
Performance
  definition   **21**
  licenses   **76, 113**
Performance, Public
  admission charge   **23**
  classroom   **21**
  definition   **21**
  library   **22**
  license agreements   **95**
  licensing agencies   **35, 113**
  music   **23**
  non-profit
    veterans or fraternal organizations   **23**
  school assemblies   **23**
Performance Rights
  agencies   **35, 113**
Permission
  forms, samples   **91–92, 94**
  writing for   **75**
Photocopying
  classroom
    multiple copies   **2, 13–14**
    single copies   **2, 13**
  current news articles   **20**
  ditto master   **20**
  for interlibrary loan   **17**
  for meetings   **19**
  for presentations   **19**
  library
    reserve use   **16**
  music   **24, 26**
  out of print materials   **18**
Photographs   **27**
  copying   **28**
  multi-media productions
    use in   **60**
Photographs, Charts and Tables
  in distance learning
    display of   **74**
Policies
  development of   **87**
  sample   **87–88**
Production Music
  copyright cleared
    sources of   **110**
Public Domain

  music   **111**
Purchase Agreements   **77**

R

Recording. *See also Multi-Media Productions*
  books   **28**
  music   **24**
    selling copies   **25**
  stories   **28**
    for the legally blind   **28**
Recording Rights
  agencies   **114**
Recordings
  instructional transmissions   **37**
  transmissions to handicapped   **38**
Records
  converting
    to tape or CD   **29**
References
  copyright law   **100**
Reserve Use
  library
    photocopying   **16**
Reserves
  library
    digital   **51**
Rights, Authors
  rights protected   **1**
  time protected   **1**

S

Satellite
  recording from   **32, 42**
Satellite Home Viewer Act of 1994   **84**
Satire
  fair use   **11**
  of TV commercial   **45**
  of TV production   **45**
  of TV program   **45**
Scanned Images
  use in multi-media productions   **63**
Screen Printing (Dump)   **54**
Searches
  copyright status of works   **75, 108**
  sources for
    addresses   **76**
Software
  computer
    archival copy   **47, 53**
    changing format   **48**
    copying from databases   **49**
    copying portions   **54**
    creating works based on other's content   **55**

databases, copying from   53
duplication of   51
hard disk, transferring programs to   48
lab pack, duplication of   53
making backups for   51
multiple machine loading   49
networking   52
Software Copyright Act of 1980   47, 49
Sonny Bono Term Extension Act   85
Spreadsheets
using data from
for multi-media productions   61
Stories
recording   28
for the legally blind   28
Student Performances
videotaping   40
Systematic reproduction
library
photocopying   15

T

TEACH Act   71–72, 86
activities not permitted   71–72
activities permitted   71–72
photographs, charts, tables
display of   74
Text
multi-media productions
use in   60
The Audio Home Recording Act of 1992   83
The Copyright Renewal Act of 1992   83
Tracing
for reproduction   27
Trademark Law   9
Transmissions
recording of
to handicapped   38

V

Video. *See also* **Video, Videocassettes, Video Programs**; *Videocassettes*
broadcasting, instructional   35–36
cable
taping from by students   43
closed circuit TV
use of   33
digital special effects   42
digitizing
placing on server   44
donated programs
use of   38
home use vs. school use versions   44

multi-media productions
use in   60
music
editing   43
off-air taping   30
at home for school use   32
closed circuit TV, use on   4, 33
for deaf & hearing impaired   31
from cable or satellite   32
retaining of tape   31
sources from which to use   30
use period   30
recordings
for instructional transmissions   37
for transmission to handicapped   38
taping student performances   40
Video Programs
after school programs
use in   45
changing formats   38
classroom use
by community members   41
by parents   41
digitizing
placing on server   44
foreign
use of   43
home use only
rental and use   39
home use vs. school use versions   44
library use   34
licensing sources
for school performance   35
loan of   42
PTA purchased
use of   43
teacher purchase or rental
use of   39
Videocassettes
after school programs
use in   45
changing formats   38
classroom use
by community members   41
by parents   41
closed circuit TV, use on   4, 33, 42
digitizing
placing on server   44
donated programs
use of   38
entertainment, use of   41
foreign
use of   43
home use only

purchasing and use   3, **34**
rental and use   3, **34**, **39**
library use   **34**
licensing sources
for school performance   **35**
loan of   **42**
PTA purchased
use of   **43**
teacher purchase or rental
use of   **39**
Videotape. *See also*
Classroom; *Video*; *Videocassettes*
off-air
closed circuit TV, use on   **4**
purchased
closed circuit TV, use on   **4**, **33**
rental
closed circuit TV, use on   **4**, **33**
Videotaping Student Performances. *See Student*
Performances

W

Warning Notices, Copyright
sample   **89**, **90**
Web Site
creation   **70**
ownership   **70**
posting magazine articles
permissibility   **73**
Work Made for Hire Act   **86**
Works
eligible for protection   **8**
not eligible for protection   **9**
World Intellectual Property Treaty (WIPO)   **81**
U.S. Copyright Law, impact on   **81**
works protected   **81**